Some Of My Best Friends Are Professors

SOME
OF MY
BEST
FRIENDS
ARE
PROFESSORS

A CRITICAL COMMENTARY
ON HIGHER EDUCATION

GEORGE WILLIAMS

ABELARD-SCHUMAN
NEW YORK & LONDON

Published by Abelard-Schuman Limited, New York and London
Manufactured in the United States of America

9498

To
3,600,000
American college students
and
their parents

CONTENTS

PREFACE

For one reason or another, I suppose I ought to mention here some matters that I would just as soon not talk about.

First, lest the reader imagine that certain skeptical comments appearing in this book, and pertaining to tests and grades, are inspired by envy, I must confess that I made absurdly good grades in college, was the second-highest man in my graduating class, and graduated *cum laude*.

Second, lest the reader imagine that this entire book is the tart fruit of a thwarted life, I must acknowledge that, though I have by no means escaped troubles and disappointments, my life has been, on the whole, far happier than that allotted to most people. On the professional side, though I am certainly not one of the "great" professors, I have taught for thirty years in what is the most highly respected university in my part of the country; I teach what I please and as I please; I am known and respected in my city and my state; I have published four books; and I have more than my quota of articles in the learned journals every year. On the personal side, my family life is unusually satisfactory; I have more good friends than I deserve; I am in excellent health; my salary is well above the national median for my academic rank, and is supplemented by royalties from my books and income from lectures; and I don't owe a dime to anybody.

The poet Housman expressed my views exactly when he said that his somewhat less than jubilant philosophy was "founded on observation of the world, not on anything so trivial and irrelevant as personal history." This book is founded on long and (in general) dispassionate observation of the university world, not on personal emotion.

Now that the book is published, only one thing bothers me. Perhaps the title should have been *Some of My Best Friends WERE Professors*. Or, still more accurately, *Some of My Best Friends Are Students*.

G. W.

Some Of My Best Friends Are Professors

WHY YOU MUST READ THIS BOOK

Within the next two or three decades, every person in the United States is certain to be personally and immediately involved in higher education in this country.

About two generations ago, in 1900, the number of men and women of college age (18 to 21) who were actually in college amounted to hardly one in 25 the country over —and in large areas of the South, the Southwest, and the West, the figure was nearer one in 100. Small children in those regions gaped at young men and women who, it was said, were college students. My own native village (population 1200) contributed, to my certain knowledge, only four students to colleges during the twelve years I lived there.

Things changed with the ending of the First World War. But even as late as 1940, only about one in ten Americans of college age were really in college. Since then, many forces (chief of which was the prosperity of the post-war years) have contributed to increasing the percentage of young people in our colleges—so that today one in three Americans of college age are in college. They number about 3,600,000 students; and their absolute number, as well as the percentage of young people going to college, is increasing steadily by approximately 200,000 per year at the time I write. Even if the percentage of those of college age who really go to college remains stable, there will be at least four and a half to five million in college by 1965, and more than seven million by 1975. Actually, however, nobody expects the percentage to remain the same. The chances are good that, by 1975, more than eight million young people will be attending our colleges.

It is easy to see why the number of young people going to college should continue to increase. The simple fact that college graduates are more numerous now than they were thirty years ago makes it possible for business and industry to demand college graduates for responsible and well-paid positions. Accordingly, the noncollege man or woman is at a serious disadvantage in the competition for jobs, and for advancement in the job he has. Young people quickly catch on to the realities of this competition, and hurry forthwith to register at the nearest available college. It is a snowballing process that may be expected to continue indefinitely.

Another reason why it may be expected to continue is that, as the number of college-educated parents grows, the number of parents who insist that their children shall attend college will grow at the same rate. No parent who has had the advantage of a college education will be content to have his own children deprived of that advantage. Furthermore, parents who have not had a college education, and who have experienced the difficulties of the noneducated in the modern world, will be almost as eager as are the college-educated to send their children to college.

I suppose no one can doubt that the financial competence of families is directly related to the likelihood of their children going to college. Of children from families with a minimum income of $8000 annually, about 98 per cent enter college; but with families having smaller incomes, the percentages fall away rapidly till, in families with incomes of $1000 annually, hardly 4 per cent of the children go to college. Urban areas have a much higher per capita income than farm areas; and the number of college students from urban families is about 400 per cent greater than the number from farm families. Within the urban areas themselves, high schools in the wealthier districts, as well as expensive private high schools, normally send over 90 per cent of their students to college, while high schools in the poorest districts are lucky if 25 per cent of their graduates go on to college. Financial competence and education go hand in hand. As long as the country can have prosperity, the percentage of young people who go to college is certain to increase.

But whether or not the country continues prosperous, the parade to the colleges seems destined to continue. The Soviet government is already subsidizing millions of college students; and the United States, in the interest of mere self-preservation, will have to do the same whenever private funds begin to fail. No alternative is possible. "We'd better take a tumble to ourselves, as the Russians have done," said Vannevar Bush recently, in commenting on the fact that the Russian government subsidizes a large percentage of its college students. "If there's a youngster with talent for science [in Russia] they make sure he gets all the education he can take." He goes on to say that the problem of America's survival is much too serious for us to adhere to the principle that a college education for young people is altogether the business of the young people and their parents, and not the business of the nation at large. In the early part of this century, college education was a luxury for the few; it is now, if we expect our nation to survive, a necessity for the many.

If the recent general prosperity fails us any further, it would be suicidal for the Federal government not to start subsidizing college students on a grand scale; indeed, many people think, with Vannevar Bush, that the United States is flirting with suicide by not instituting Federal subsidization of college students today. Such subsidization would be no new thing in American history. In the 1930's about 620,000 college students were aided materially by the Federal government. Currently many thousands of college students are receiving substantial subsidization through their participation in the Army and Navy ROTC programs. The Office of Vocational Rehabilitation is providing substantial assistance to the several states in order to help educate disabled civilians. And several branches of the health services, the Department of Agriculture, the Atomic Energy Commission, and other governmental agencies are subsidizing graduate students in many universities. The G.I. educational benefits, only recently abandoned, offered aid to millions of college students. In other words, the precedent for personal financial aid to college students has already been established. It would be unrealistic to believe that, in case of either a depression like that of the 1930's or even a slight warming up of the cold war with Russia, the government would not undertake a large-scale program of assistance to college students.

Under President Truman, a Commission on Higher

Education (whose members included Arthur H. Compton, Milton Eisenhower, Douglas S. Freeman, Bishop Oxnam, Rabbi Wise, and twenty-five other prominent Americans) reported: "Recognizing the economic difficulties which will preclude many qualified students from entering college, this Commission recommends that a national program of Federal Scholarships in the form of grants-in-aid be provided for at least 20 per cent of all undergraduate, nonveteran students." At that time (1947) the Commission recommended that Federal aid for college students be made on the basis of ability and of "individual need."

Ten years later, after the difficulties with Russia had become more serious, another Presidential Committee on Education Beyond the High School, recognizing the relationship between college education and national survival, made elaborate recommendations for Federal aid to college students. These recommendations did not include direct grants to college students in addition to the grants already being made. Direct aid should be left as much as possible, the Committee thought, to the colleges themselves, to the individual states, and to private benefactors. Nevertheless, the Committee recognized that the nation is obligated, in terms of national defense, to see that the potential brain-power of young America is fully developed. In short, if private individuals and non-Federal agencies find themselves unable to assure college education for increasing numbers of our young people, the Federal government will be compelled to assist. Whether or not we like this prospect, we are going to have to accept it as a possibility for the immediate future —unless we prefer to accept the prospect of certain destruction of this nation. All this means that, however we look at the problem, and whatever our private opinions may be, the population of our colleges is certain to keep growing.

But can we find young people of ability in sufficient numbers to allow our colleges to continue expanding? The answer is an emphatic yes. Apparently the Russians have found no dearth of good material among their young people; and there is no evidence that young people in the United States are any stupider than those in the Soviet Union. Even now we are not sending all our best young brains to college. For example, a study by Professor Byron Hollinshead, published in 1953, indicated that "only two-fifths of American youth within the top quarter of intellectual ability are attending college." Poverty (even in the prosperous 1950's) keeps one fifth of the highest-ranking young people out of college; and failure of the colleges (or of society) to make the colleges sufficiently attractive keeps out another fifth. (Personal factors, such as marriage, desire to make money in order to marry, family disagreements, desire to enter the armed forces, pressure from parents who want to keep the child at home, bad health, and so on account for the remaining one fifth.)

Even these figures, however, do not reflect the possibilities for the future. If it is true that virtually all the children of wealthy parents go to college, we may assume that, in a nation in which all parents were prosperous, virtually all children would be college material. It is almost as simple as that. Given every educational opportunity and incentive from childhood onward through two generations (or about 65 years), at least four fifths of all the nation's children might be expected eventually to go to college. Such a percentage will probably not be reached during the present century; but (barring a national disaster) it will almost certainly be reached in the twenty-first century. This prediction is based on the following facts: the snowballing quality, already mentioned, of the demand for college graduates can hardly be expected to diminish in an increasingly complex and technological society; the long, unbroken trend in America for more and more people to get more and more education will probably not reverse itself—if it did, it would mean that the country considers ignorance more valuable than knowledge, which is an inconceivable concession; the natural human love, pride, ambition, and jealousy that make every parent want his child to have the best available educational opportunities will continue as long as parents remain human; the age-old trend of all human societies to prolong the educational period of their young cannot be expected to end; and the responsibility felt by government and society at large for the welfare of all individuals within the society is much more likely to increase, rather than decrease, in the future.

In any event, nobody can doubt that, in the generation just ahead of us, every family in America, and almost every individual in America, will be, at some time, immediately and personally involved in the life of some college. In turn, and as a result of the college involvements of so many individuals at the most impressionable period of their lives, the colleges themselves will exercise an influence on national life that can hardly be overestimated. Political philosophy and economic theory, religious beliefs and moral ideals, social customs and personal values, literature and art, law and punishment, individual ambitions and national aspirations—all will be directly or indirectly affected by the colleges, and by the points of view they uphold in their own right or inculcate in their students.

What is more, this vast expansion is going to cost money—oceans of money—for buildings, laboratories, equipment, libraries, upkeep, salaries of professors. By 1975 our colleges will be costing us at least $50 billion annually, and much more later on, as the colleges grow. Most of this money will be derived from state and Federal taxes, and relatively little from the private largess of individual donors. The would-be philanthropic donors will be so hard pressed by taxes to support public education that they will have little left over to bestow on private education. In other words, even that small part of the population that never sees what the ivied walls look like from the inside will be forced to participate in college life by contributing larger and larger sums to support the colleges.

What I have tried to say in these few pages is that the colleges of America are certain to become, within a relatively few years, immensely more populous than they now are, as well as immensely more influential in American life, and of intimate personal concern to every American.

It seems indisputable, therefore, that every American owes it to himself, his family, his country, his civilization, and perhaps the human race itself to take a long appraising look at American colleges. It is curious that not many people either outside or inside college walls have ever taken such a look at our colleges. Whether because of popular awe or popular indifference, American colleges have been singularly free to develop just as they pleased. Perhaps the reason for the general public unconcern has been that only a minute fraction of the people have been intimately involved with the colleges in the past. At any rate, except for a few perfunctory, publicity-seeking gestures made at rare intervals by certain state legislators, or a few nominal demands by church groups, nobody outside the colleges has seriously tried to find out what the colleges are actually doing, whether they ought to be doing it, what they ought to be doing, and whether they are doing well, or can be induced to do well, what they ought to be doing. Everything has been left to the colleges themselves.

This outside neglect might be commendable if the colleges themselves were inclined to indulge in self-analysis or self-criticism at a level more than skin-deep. Unfortunately, however, the self-analysis and self-criticism to which the colleges subject themselves begins with the assumption that the colleges as they now exist are basically sound, and that all they need is a certain amount of regular screw-tightening here and there, and an occasional new paint and polish job. The more daring and original minds among the professors are absorbed in their research, and consider teaching a necessary nuisance; and the less daring and original minds have been long warped into conventional patterns that cannot be broken. As a result, the colleges, considered *as educational institutions* and not as promoters of research, considered *as teaching instruments* and not as places where new discoveries are made in science and (more especially) in scholarship, are almost universally faint-hearted, indifferent, and backward. In the forty years that I have been associated with colleges, as student and teacher, I have seen no significant changes in educational methods or attitudes. It is conceivable, of course, that the colleges arrived at the best of all possible stages forty years ago, and that any subsequent change would have been for the worse. But this is doubtful.

The only changes that have occurred (except in the numbers of students on the campus) have seldom involved anything but a shuffling of credits required for graduation, a revaluation of certain courses in terms of semester hours, the introduction or the elimination of certain "required" courses, new systems for determining whether a student shall "go on probation" or receive "honors," the adoption of some Tweedledum textbook to replace a Tweedledee textbook, or (if the college is exceedingly progressive) the hesitant and soul-searching introduction of an occasional "experimental" course or program of study.

In the days when the colleges affected only a tiny fraction of the population, it did not much matter what they did—whether they stagnated or progressed, whether they taught well or ill. But the time is upon us when it does matter. Very soon the vast majority of Americans will go to college; those who do not go will have children who go; and every man and woman will be paying stiff taxes to help support the colleges. It is essential, therefore, that the American college be examined carefully with a view to our discovering whether it is worthy of the destiny it has just before it, as well as of the trust we must put in it as the chief defender of our nation and of our civilization in the days to come.

CHAPTER TWO

THE FAILURE OF THE UNIVERSITIES

Failure by University Standards

With the appearance of the Russian *sputnik* in the autumn
of 1957, many angry remarks about the failure of American science blistered the American atmosphere. The
American universities, which apparently had not developed scientists who could compete with the Russians in
the matter of launching *sputniks,* were not left entirely
unsinged by the blistering remarks. Whether or not these
criticisms of American universities were justified, or
whether producing scientists who can produce *sputniks* is the highest ideal to which a university may
aspire, is a difficult problem that will not be considered
here. Nevertheless, certain facts do suggest that American
universities are failing rather badly—even by their own
standards, to say nothing of the standards held by people
outside the ivied walls. This does not mean that the universities are *complete* failures; it means merely that they
are far more unsuccessful, according to their own standards, than they are generally willing to admit.

One criterion of success may be the opinion of students
in the institutions of higher learning. In a four-volume

study called *Adventure in Education,* published about fifteen years ago, it was found that, of 3600 men and women students examined, only about 43 per cent were thoroughly satisfied with their colleges; only 18 per cent had acquired "a deep and abiding interest in learning"; only 10 per cent had acquired an "intelligent interest in contemporary affairs"; and only 5 per cent had acquired "knowledge of useful methods of work."

In another study, by Professor Franz Schneider, at the University of California, of professor-ratings by 1620 students, it was found that only 10 per cent of the professors were rated as excellent, 37 per cent were rated as fair, and 53 per cent were rated as poor. These figures reflect pretty well my own experiences with colleagues who have had children in college, often in the same college where their fathers taught. These children have had the advantage of professional, and often intimately informed, advice in the choice of professors and courses. Nevertheless, almost every one of these professor-fathers whom I have consulted has admitted that at least half the professors under whom his children studied were incompetent.

Another suggestive criterion of university success is the number of students who fail out of the university. This number is usually classified information. But we can obtain some estimate of the number failing from all causes by knowing that any one graduating class is usually only about 60 per cent to 65 per cent as large as it was when it entered as as a freshman class. The 35 per cent to 40 per cent who do not graduate do not necessarily represent failures: some students leave college on account of illness, some on account of financial troubles, some because they have acquired outside interests. Nevertheless, we should not be far wrong in estimating that the colleges are absolute and total failures in trying to educate about 20 per cent to 30 per cent of the students they originally accepted, or selected, as hopeful prospects. The fact that the figures are no better, and are often worse, in those institutions that have rigorous selective procedures for their freshmen does not make the institutions look any more successful.

Naturally, the universities like to say that it is the student, not the student's university, that has failed. More will be said about this matter later on. It may be worth mentioning here, however, that about 200,000 of the students in the upper fourth of their high school graduating class who enter college drop out subsequently *of their own volition* because they feel that college has nothing for them that is worth the trouble of obtaining. This 200,000 constitute material as good as any college can expect; yet the colleges fail to give them a "higher education."

Besides the students who enter college and then drop out, or fail, one must count the many students who (according to the colleges' own standards) barely escape being technical failures—those students who are in continual scholastic hot water, failing a few courses, changing their majors because of unsuccess, going on probation, repeating courses, failing out of college and returning for another try the next year, requiring five or six years to graduate, transferring to other colleges, and so on. These virtual failures run to something between 10 per cent and 20 per cent each year for most colleges. All told, therefore, the colleges (by their own standards) fail with one third to one half of their students. It is a startling record of inefficiency.

As a matter of fact, even this record presents the colleges in an undeservedly favorable light. Almost any professor in almost any university will tell you that if, in a class of twenty undergraduates, he has two students who are altogether satisfactory—students who learn what he teaches them quite as well as he could wish—he considers himself lucky. The other 90 per cent of the class range from partial to total failures. Some years ago Professor Raymond L. Garnett made a study of freshmen at the University of Missouri. His conclusion was this: "On the basis for success adopted for this study, 40.2 per cent of the 876 students included in the study met with success during their first year." That is to say, approximately 60 per cent were failures. (In this study the basis on which a student was judged "successful" was the "minimum degree of scholarship which will permit a student to be graduated.") All things considered, therefore, it would seem that the colleges are unsuccessful in satisfactorily educating at least half of their students. This is an extremely liberal estimate; the real figure is probably pretty close to that 18 per cent (mentioned earlier) who acquire in college "a deep and abiding interest in learning."

Turning from the failures and looking at the successes, we reach the same results. Recently, Professors Robert H. Knapp and Joseph J. Greenbaum made an exhaustive study of the collegiate origins of *The Younger American Scholar*. They found that, of about 800 American institutions granting the bachelor's degree, only about 50 produce male scholars in excess of 10 per 1000, and that the range among these 50 institutions is from 10 to 60 per 1000. These writers conclude that the production of scholars seems "to leave undeveloped large segments of the American system of higher education." In other words, about 93 per cent of American institutions of higher learning are doing a poor job producing scholars that satisfy collegiate standards of scholarship.

Failure by Other Standards

By standards of success other than those of the colleges themselves, the showing the colleges make may be even poorer. It is notorious that the colleges did not recognize the abilities, elicit the best work, or inspire the interest of this century's two greatest men—Winston Churchill and Franklin Roosevelt, both of whom made worse than mediocre records in college. President Eisenhower was not (to put it gently) a brilliant student before he went to West Point, and at West Point he was only number 61 in a graduating class of 168. President Truman never attended college. President Hoover made an excellent record (in engineering) at college—but he was also one of the least successful of our presidents. Of America's more important literary figures, Robert Frost was a notoriously bad student in college; William Faulkner and John Steinbeck attended college, but found no permanent satisfactions there, and took no degrees; Hemingway never went to college; Edna St. Vincent Millay was suspended; Sinclair Lewis had such difficulties at Yale that he dropped out for some time; F. Scott Fitzgerald was a resounding failure at Princeton; Thomas Wolfe did well at college, but wrote contemptuously of college all his life; Vachel Lindsay entered college, did poorly, and left without graduating; Edgar Lee Masters, Edwin Arlington Robinson, and Wallace Stevens all attended college, but did not stay to graduate. In England, Nobel Prize winners Kipling, Yeats, and Shaw never attended college; neither did the Poet Laureate Masefield, nor did Walter de la Mare. The poets Noyes, Sassoon, and Spender went to the university, but took no degrees. Cataloguing like this could go on indefinitely. What it proves is that the college does not necessarily attract, inspire, or recognize genius.

Even on a plane lower than genius, success in college is not a prerequisite for what most people (including the colleges themselves) would call "success." For example, among the trustees or regents now running most of America's colleges, Phi Beta Kappas are exceedingly uncommon. In matters of mere money-making, college is notoriously unessential: Henry Ford, Jesse Jones, Hugh Roy Cullen, Sid Richardson (reputed to be the richest man in America) never went to college. John R. Tunis' book on what happened to the 541 graduates of Harvard, 1911, is well known. Twenty-three of these graduates were mentioned in *Who's Who*. Of these, only six were Phi Beta Kappas. The others were athletes (two), men-about-campus (six), and a "nondescript group that failed in any special manner to distinguish itself in college . . . just run-of-the-mill undergraduates."

Actually, it seems probable that colleges discourage those qualities that we associate with original genius. The colleges have seldom ventured to investigate this problem. But one study (by J. W. Riley, *et al.*) showed that students themselves, at any rate, feel that the college faculty discourages independent thinking; and a separate study (by Professor Daniel Harris) of 456 freshmen at City College, New York, showed that low grades in college were associated with "nonconformity," "literary inclinations," and comparatively good grades in English and in studies dealing with human nature and human society.

Of course, the colleges will answer that many students who have been successful by college standards have been successful by other standards as well. This is quite true.

But when we balance the names of these people against those of other great or successful men who were not recognized or inspired by the colleges they attended, or who did not attend college, and still others who were phenomenally successful by college standards but have not been heard of since, we are compelled to say that a student's success in college seems to have no positive relation to major achievement outside college. That is to say, the colleges seem to have been seeking something, valuing something, encouraging something, measuring something, and recognizing something besides the things in a student's character that make for major achievement. Indeed, not only do they fail to perceive and to bring out latent potentialities, but they also seem even to repel, and often to stifle, the exceptionally original and capable. It seems that some students may possess traits which colleges value, and possess also traits that make for major achievement. But the two sets of traits are not identical, and are often contradictory.

To this the colleges may reply that they are not interested in developing traits that make for major achievement or for a "successful" life in the world outside the colleges, or for full realization of the students' highest potentialities as persons or as citizens; that their only interest is in developing excellent scholars who can learn what they are taught, and then go on and learn more and teach more. If this is so—it should not be so. This ideal amounts to hardly more than the ambition to train people to become professors who will train other people to become professors who will train other people to become professors. . . . Surely the function of the colleges in the modern world is something higher than that. If not, or even if that be their major function, then the nation as a whole, the parents of the nation, and the young people of the nation will simply have to find some other kind of agency to do educational justice to the young people.

As a matter of fact, the colleges fail in attaining even this ideal of scholarship among their students (if it *is* an ideal). The professors themselves are continually complaining that most of their students, after leaving college, do not continue the scholarly habits they may have acquired in college, read nothing of value, write nothing, do no research, spend their leisure time looking at television or going to night clubs or attending cocktail parties or playing bridge or entertaining at the country club, have no scholarly or artistic or scientific hobbies, and become in general the thoroughly nonintellectual, nonscholarly, nonscientific upper-middle-class American who has been the despair of thinking people since the days of Mencken and Sinclair Lewis.

It is no credit to the colleges that most of their graduates become avid readers of the *Saturday Evening Post,* the *Reader's Digest,* the *Ladies' Home Journal,* and *Time* —and not much of anything else. It is no compliment to the colleges that many ardent supporters of Senator McCarthy were college graduates.* It is no compliment to the colleges that, throughout the South, the most influential opponents of racial segregation are college graduates editing newspapers or practicing law or serving as judges or legislators. It is no compliment to the colleges that a very large proportion of the college-trained professional men in the nation constitute the nucleus of reaction in the nation. It is no compliment to the colleges that, among

---

* Gallup polls in 1953 showed that 42 per cent of college-educated people were "favorable" to McCarthy, 50 per cent were "unfavorable," and 8 per cent were "undecided."

the millions of young people who have graduated from college during the last few years, it is next to impossible to carry on a conversation except about business, household affairs, or last evening's television program. It is no compliment to the colleges that 90 per cent of those alumni who may continue through the years to be concerned with the fortunes of their college, are concerned almost exclusively with the fortunes of its athletic teams.

Failure in Success

By almost any of the standards mentioned, the colleges fail with the majority of their students. But even with their admitted successes, one may question whether they have succeeded in the right ways. A good summary of what the American system of education has achieved is that of Professor Sidney Hook, in the following passages —for though he is referring chiefly to the precollege schools of America, his words apply equally well to the colleges. With pride and approval, Professor Hook lists the major achievements of our educational system:

> 1. The American school and educational system has been the prime agency of achieving a unified democratic nation out of diverse ethnic groups of varied national origins.

Undoubtedly the achievement of such democracy as exists in America has been furthered by American schools. But (disregarding the fact that pure democracy is hardly so universally admired, among either faculty or students, as Professor Hook implies) one pauses at the word *unified*. Certainly, for the nation to be unified in defense of the spirit of democracy is an ideal above all praise. But *unified* is too much like *uniformized, standardized,* and *con-*

ventionalized to be an unmixed blessing. The more a society is unified, the more likely it is to offer official opposition to individual freedom, individual variation from the general norms of behavior, individual deviation from the popular patterns of thought. The one thing upon which liberals and conservatives, radicals and reactionaries would agree is that, as the American nation has become "unified," individual freedom, variation, and deviation have become increasingly difficult to maintain, increasingly dangerous to practice. There is peril in the word "unified."

> 2. The American educational system has provided an educational ladder on which millions have climbed to a better social life.

If Professor Hook means by "better social life" that American education has helped Americans achieve a "higher standard of living"—better food, better health, better working conditions, more leisure, more security in sickness and in age, more prosperity generally—then we can heartily agree that this achievement has been worth while. But if he admires the "unified," standardized, conformist, materialistic life of most middle-class Americans, in which the chief ideal is a new and longer automobile every year, a new and bigger deep-freeze, a television set for every room, a well-stocked home bar, and membership in a country club, and if he thinks that American education is to be praised for having helped Americans achieve this kind of life—one must again register a question as to the unqualified success of American education.

> 3. . . . it has remained neutral in the great conflicts of religious faiths.

Is this good or bad? For though it is true that every

man should be allowed to hold and to practice whatever religious faith he wishes, it does not follow that the schools, and especially the colleges and universities, should be neutral in religious matters. Colleges and universities should be allowed—no, encouraged—to express, through their professors, scholarly and scientific opinions about religion. Much of what passes in our democracy for religious faith is a deliberate refusal on the part of "religious" people to assume the responsibility of solving the world's terrifying problems, and a dependence instead upon the theory that "God will take care of you"; still more of the current American enthusiasm for religion is exhibitionism and ignorance; and much of it is based on notions that are historically false, scientifically unsound, and philosophically primitive. It is not to the credit of the educational system, and especially the colleges and universities, that it "has remained neutral" on such matters.

4. . . . it has come nearest to achieving a classless school system in the entire history of human society. *Morally* this is a most glorious achievement.

This again deserves a hearty cheer. But Professor Hook continues:

Educationally, this [classless school system] has created prodigious difficulties and theoretical confusions.

Many of the difficulties and confusions in the colleges and universities are due to that schizophrenic trait that will often be mentioned in this book. An increasing number of educators, uncomfortably aware of the failures of the higher educational system, and refusing to blame the colleges and universities themselves, as well as the professors, for the failure, are beginning to preach, as President Conant did, that the university, as a teaching agency, is "concerned with professional education . . . and the general education of the leading citizens." In opposition to the formidable group that believes in this ideal —the ideal of more and more exclusive and selective colleges and universities—many other educators and citizens at large are demanding more and more education for *all* young people. Though I think (for reasons listed in the first chapter of this book) that the latter group of educators will win, they will not win easily. Those who believe in the aristocratic ideal of education, that is, education for the elite alone, are finding supporters everywhere. This ideal, however, implies a complete denial of the very heart of democratic theory, and is also a rationalization in which the colleges and universities indulge in order to conceal from themselves their own failures, and to avoid the painful self-analysis, self-criticism, and self-reconstruction that they need so badly.

At this point let me summarize what has been said so far in this chapter. First, the colleges and universities fail outright, according to their own standards, with from one third to one half the students they enroll. And they succeed outright, according to their own standards, with only about 10 to 15 per cent of the students they enroll. The remaining students prove by their conduct subsequent to graduation that, for the most part, they never attain the university ideal of true education. By other than university standards, the records do not show that institutions of higher education have been generally capable of recognizing, attracting, inspiring, or nourishing greatness of character or nonprofessorial abilities. Furthermore, some of the major achievements on which our educational system prides itself are open to some grave criticisms. On the whole, therefore, the American college and university cannot be considered a highly successful enterprise.

The Universities Are Not Total Failures

In spite of all that has been said here, however, it must be remembered that the colleges and universities are not *total* failures. If I have left that impression, I should be very sorry. They succeed in two ways.

First, they succeed (by their own standards) with the 10 to 15 per cent mentioned above; and they succeed to varying extents with the remaining third to half of their students—that is, the ones who are not total failures.

Second, there is a negative success which, ironically, may be the chief contribution of the colleges and universities to the education of their students. For four impressionable years of their lives, when the characters they will have as adults are finally being shaped, the students are kept cloistered from the more deleterious influences within our society. That is, the young people are kept from rubbing elbows with crime, vice, dishonesty, ignorance, commercialism, disorderly thinking, cheapness of taste, and brutality of action, all of which are widespread in the world outside the campus. This negative contribution of higher education is itself sufficient to justify the four years spent on the campus. It should be argument enough against those who would reserve the campus for the selected elite, and nobody else. Indeed, it is almost true that the selected elite need the advantages of college and university *less* than anybody else in the country.

In this negative contribution, the colleges and universities do much good. The only real quarrel anybody can have with them on this score is that negative good is not enough. The colleges and universities are like a farmer who cultivates land from which he harvests only 10 bushels of wheat per acre. We cannot quarrel with the 10 bushels; it is better than nothing. But it falls far short of the 60 bushels that the farmer ought to be producing. The impression that I should like this chapter to leave is that (with some few exceptions to be mentioned later in this book) the American college or university is not an evil institution; it is a good institution that is something like 10 to 20 per cent as good as it could be and ought to be.

CHAPTER THREE

THE NATURAL HISTORY OF THE PROFESSOR

From the first it should be admitted that any book (like this one) which speaks of the "university professor" as a species, or of the "typical university professor," is certain to be inaccurate and unfair to many professors as individuals. No single one of them is like any generalized picture of the "university professor," and many of them are not typical. Nevertheless, it is perfectly possible to make sound generalizations about professors as a class. It is like saying, "The typical American automobile cost its owner less than $3000." For even though one sees Cadillacs and Lincolns every day, they are *not* the typical automobile of America's roads and streets. After carefully considering all the professors I have ever known, and trying to be as just as human nature can be, I am convinced that the following remarks are true of not less than two thirds, and more probably four fifths, of all the professors I have known.

Self-Satisfaction on the Campus

The university professor sits at the apex of the vast educational pyramid in America, respected by parents, by teachers in the public schools, by students, and by alumni. For my own part, I am often touched, in professional meetings with high school teachers, to observe the extraordinary faith that these good people have in university professors. At these meetings I have felt as a feudal lord must feel among peasants; and sometimes I blush to find that, in spite of myself, I "Assume the god, / Affect to nod / And seem to shake the spheres." The high school teacher struggles hard to make his standards meet those set by the university professors, and never thinks to ask whether those standards represent a sound educational ideal.

All this is particularly ironical in view of the fact that, in the better universities, the professors do not like to think of themselves as, primarily, teachers, but as scholars and scientists. Later on I shall have something to say about the professor in his very important function as scholar or scientist; but just now I wish to consider him in his function as teacher. After all, as Professor F. M. Rogers of Harvard has said, "Universities are organized as teaching institutions . . . They are endowed as teaching institutions. Parents pay their offspring's university fees, and of this there can be no doubt, because universities are teaching institutions." Professors draw their salaries as teachers; and excessively rare are the scholars and scientists whom any American university is willing to support without demanding certain teaching duties in return. Yet professors are universally reluctant to assume responsibility for any of those really monstrous failures in teaching such as were briefly mentioned in the preceding chapter.

An example of what I mean appears in the student newspaper of my own university this very day. This university selects its freshmen with the utmost care — by means of batteries of many kinds of tests, personal recommendations, interviews, and so on. Hardly one in five candidates who have the temerity to apply for admission is accepted; the faculty-student ratio is very high; the university is inexpensive, does not accept students who are not solvent enough to get along without financial difficulty, and has innumerable scholarships for even fairly mediocre students. But in today's student newspaper the registrar of the university, a kind and dedicated man, pointed out that only 57.8 per cent of the students who enter the university as freshmen eventually graduate. Then he went on to say: "I am convinced that there are very few students entering the university who are incapable of handling the work. No one fails out because of lack of ability. I would say that most of the fail-outs stem from personal adjustments that the student fails to make."

This is most revealing. It tends to confirm, from an authority who has his finger on the pulse of the university, the point of view maintained throughout this book — namely, that the failure of the American university to educate properly a large majority of its students is not due, as a general thing, to grave and widespread lack of ability among high school graduates who have been accepted into the university. At the same time, the registrar's statement is sadly typical of the almost invariable unwillingness of professors everywhere to blame themselves, or the university, or the methods of the university, for the students' failures. This particular case is uniquely notable since the registrar cannot, in view of the university's rigid entrance requirements, low cost, and financial solvency of the students, lay the blame for the large percentage of failures on student unpreparedness or unintelligence. The "personal adjustments that the student fails to make" probably involve an absolute minimum of family difficulties and financial problems. By far the greater part of these personal adjustments must, therefore, involve the student and the university directly. Since the part of the university that most affects the student, the one with which he comes into most consistent contact, and the one which he is quite powerless to change, is the faculty, the registrar's statement means, essentially, that the students have difficulty adjusting to the faculty. And since the students are admittedly able young people, the whole thing boils down to the fact that some unusually bright students cannot adjust to their professors. It would seem that, under the circumstances, the professors, as the leaders in the university community, and the people to whom the students naturally look for guidance, might occasionally wonder whether they themselves are not largely to blame for the students' failure to make adjustments to the university. Yet I have never heard any professor in my university assume an iota of blame for the absolute failure of 42.2 per cent of the students, to say nothing of the 10 to 15 per cent who are virtual failures, and the 25 to 30 per cent who are partial failures. Just this year, for example, when the freshman class, having been selected by the most rigorous procedures ever used by the university, made one of the poorest academic records in the history of the university, the chief administrative officer explained "this year's freshman class is better qualified to do the work than any previous class here, and its low grades are due to 'playing' and not concentrating on studies." This is the invariable attitude of professors everywhere: when students fail, it is strictly the student's fault. This universal attitude of professors and of administrations is exactly the same as if they should say that the tragedies in the lives of Hamlet, King Duncan, and Desdemona "stem from personal adjustments that these characters fail to make."

I have spent time analyzing the situation in my own university because conditions here are more favorable for student success than in most other institutions of higher learning. Admission of "poorly prepared" students, desire for quantity enrollment, pressures from outside influences, and admission of students without careful personal selection are all reduced to a minimum. Within the university itself the faculty-student ratio is high, the reputation of the faculty is excellent, library facilities and conditions of study are superior. Yet 42.2 per cent of the students fail, and the professors refuse to assume any particle of the blame.

This dodging of responsibility is more than typical; it is practically universal among professors in all universities. One never expects anything else. In all the faculty meetings or departmental meetings I have attended in more than thirty years of teaching, I have heard one professor say on one occasion that one problem, at that time troubling the faculty, might be due to poor teaching. The only result of this suggestion was a shocked faculty and the professor's acquiring a reputation as a dangerous radical.

A few years ago an investigating committee (composed of Professors A. E. Severinghaus and H. J. Carman of Columbia, and W. E. Cadbury of Haverford) published a volume called *Preparation for Medical Education in the Liberal Arts College* (1953). The committee was not so much concerned with preparation for medical education in a restricted sense as with good liberal education. After studying 114 colleges in the United States and Canada, the committee, in a chapter on "The Teacher and His Methods," reached this conclusion: "If what we saw is a representative cross section of teacher performance, the majority of our college teachers fall far short of the level of teaching effectiveness they could attain." One reviewer described this chapter as a "devastating evaluation and indictment of college teaching in general." Lack of self-criticism among professors, the committee thought, was one reason for the low level of college teaching. "There is unconfessed reluctance to undertake the painful, dismaying, and divisive task of self-examination."

Proving this last statement statistically would be difficult. Nevertheless, I can testify from my own experience that professors in general and colleges and universities as a whole have neither changed their methods of instruction appreciably nor their entire intellectual approach to the problem of teaching, since I was a freshman nearly forty years ago. Obviously, self-satisfaction has reigned on the campus all these years, and just as obviously, it is still present. Among the faculty on every university campus that I know, I note an almost universal self-satisfaction and a universal lack of self-criticism. In a small effort to get some actual statistics on this topic, I have just made a quick little investigation of my own. I have looked over the circulation records of the relatively few books in my own university library that might conceivably interest any teacher hoping to improve his work. I selected books acquired by the library over the last thirty years, and chose the seventy-five books that seemed to me to offer the most promise of help. I found that, during the thirty years, about half of these books had never been taken from the library even once, and that the average number of borrowings per book for the thirty-year period was just under one. This is, of course, a very rough check. On the other hand, since most of the borrowings were certainly by students and professors in the Education department, the figure of less than one borrowing in thirty years does more than ample justice to the educational researches of professors in other departments. At any rate, the figures do not reveal any burning enthusiasm on the part of the faculty to learn about teaching.

W. C. Eells' comprehensive bibliography of writings on *College Teachers and College Teaching* (1957) has just become available. Under the heading "Teaching Methods" (which includes all items about the problems of actual teaching), Eells lists 70 American books larger than pamphlet size (60 pages) published in the twelve years before 1957. Of these books, 30 are surveys or reports describing existing conditions; 19 deal with the potentialities of "audio-visual" education (a field in which some professors have actually been trying to make some advances, usually against the scornful opposition of nearly all other professors); and the remaining 21 deal with the actual problems of instruction. These 21 books are distributed over different fields as follows: social sciences, 4; nursing, 3; foreign languages, 2; reading, 2; religion, 2; medicine, 1; engineering, 1 (86 pages in 1950); certain community teaching experiments, 3; the large problems of teaching, 3. Only these last three books seriously consider the really fundamental problems and responsibilities of the college teacher, his approach to his profession, his attitude toward his students, his methods of sharing knowledge, his relation to the culture of his time, and his ethics as a teacher, a man, and an American. It will be noted, furthermore, that not one of the books deals with the problems of teaching the "solid" subjects of mathematics, physics, chemistry, biology, geology, history, philosophy, or English.

But though the books on teaching, when examined closely, are not numerous, published articles average about seventy per year for the twelve years covered in the bibliography. But here again, a closer look reveals less actual concern with the problems of teaching than would at first appear. For one thing, a large number of these articles are written by professors of education and educational psychology, not by professors in the actual field of discussion. Next, many of the articles consist of not much more than scholarly platitudes (by college administrators and retiring presidents of learned societies whose speeches are reprinted in the "Proceedings") on large, vague, safe topics that everybody is for: God, home, country, culture, democracy, larger endowments for universities, and larger salaries for teachers. Third, an astonishingly large number of them are gently satirical essays, written with plaintive humor, by professors who confess to having finally resigned themselves to the futility of their lot. And fourth, a few of them describe pet teaching projects that, while commendably original, are applicable only to certain peculiar conditions. It would probably be fair to say that about 20 to 25 articles per year are directed toward self-criticism and self-improvement among college professors, and might conceivably help somebody else teach. In terms of personalities involved, fewer than 70 (one in three thousand) college professors and administrators per year write articles on the problems of teaching, and only about 20 (one in ten thousand) write articles showing genuine self-criticism and eagerness for the fundamental betterment of college teaching.

I realize that many college professors who do not publish articles on teaching may be, nevertheless, self-critical and eager to be better teachers. On the other hand, I suppose we have a right to assume that those professors who do publish articles on teaching are fairly representative of those who don't. Our interest, then, turns to the articles themselves as representing the type of self-criticism and of progressive thinking to be found among the professors.

My own feeling is that at least ninety-nine per cent of the authors are only toying with the fringes of the real problem. This feeling arises from two facts. One of these facts has already been noted: the colleges have not appreciably changed their methods of instruction or their attitudes toward students and student psychology in at least forty years. The other fact is that, since 1930, or even 1945, the most extraordinary changes have occurred in the American system of values and ways of life.

Among the changes that have occurred, we must surely reckon an unprecedented sense of insecurity. "There is only one question," says William Faulkner. "When will I be blown up? . . . Our tragedy today is a general and universal physical fear." Another change involves our young people. It is undeniable that a spirit of cynicism, lawlessness, contempt for authority, contempt for the older generation, and universal disobedience has infected them. In society as a whole, there has been a steep decline of religious belief among very large numbers of people, especially among the better educated; and even those people who are still religious do not hold, for the most part, to the orthodoxies of their parents. There can be no doubt that the individual has lost significance except in relation to society, and that contemporary law is directed far more toward accomplishing the welfare of society than the welfare of the individual. Our old sexual and moral standards have been shattered. Our old political faiths have been assailed or conquered by doctrines that would have been unthinkable in 1900. Urbanization and accompanying changes in domestic manners are occurring at dizzying speeds. Millions of Americans have traveled abroad, and brought back new sets of values that would have horrified their grandparents. Our old concepts of psychology and of personality have been turned inside out.

Yet the colleges are still trying to teach as they did in the early part of this century — and the best that the typical professor can do to adjust higher education to this new age of terrifying and stupendous change is to write articles (I choose titles at random) on "The Practicum Examination in Botany and Biology," "Teaching College Grammar by Induction and Deduction," "The Place of the Undergraduate Thesis in Engineering Education," "Frequent Testing as a Motivating Factor in Large Literature Classes," "The Competitive Lecture-Quiz Cheatproof Examination," and so on. If Nero became infamous for fiddling while Rome burned, what will be the future reputation of the modern college professor?

I have come across one writer of articles who seems to understand the problem of adjusting higher education to the new age. This is Professor C. Page Smith of California and he writes: "Modern education has its roots in a world view born in the eighteenth century and elaborated . . . in the nineteenth century. This Enlightenment view of the world . . . is no longer adequate to the needs of modern man . . . A change will come in both school and college when the now obsolete metaphysic of the Enlightenment is replaced by a more human sociology which exposes the failures of the present system and shows them to be an intolerable affront to the human spirit and a vulgarization of the whole process of education."

Perhaps I should explain briefly, for the benefit of those who have not recently studied the Enlightenment, a few of the things which this philosophy implied. It assumed that all men possess a special faculty of "reason" which, if relied upon, would cause all men to see "truth" exactly alike, and react to it uniformly; but today's psychology reveals that no man possesses such a faculty, and that no two people can possibly react in the same manner to the same thing, and that professorial attempts to make students react alike to knowledge is "an affront to the human spirit." The Enlightenment implied, as does the typical college professor in his class, that "truth" is definitive, absolute, well recognized, identical for all people, and attainable by all serious-minded and industrious people; but modern philosophy reveals that "truth" (except sometimes among the concrete facts of nature) is relative, variable, dependent on circumstances, and always a receding vision to him who advances toward it. The Enlightenment believed, as does our college professor in his teaching, that anybody who chooses to do so can find "truth" and behave in a "moral" and "rational" manner merely by exercising "self-discipline" and not "playing around"; but modern psychiatry reveals that self-determination is largely an illusion for young people, and that the nature of an individual and his reactions to the world are decided not so much by "self-discipline" as by inescapable

outside influences, the experiences of a lifetime unconscious fears and desires, and physiological peculiarities
over which "self-discipline" has no control. The Enlightenment believed, as does the modern professor lecturing his ever-failing students, that every individual is a
self-sufficient and independent entity that may say truth-
fully of itself, "I am the master of my fate"; but modern
sociology knows that no person can possibly be free of
the overwhelming influences exercised by his society, his
cultural surroundings, and his age in history. The Enlightenment believed, as does the grade-giving and self-
satisfied modern professor, that those individuals who
fail to come to terms with man's inevitably upward-
tending destiny do so of their own free will and stubborn-
ness, and are justly judged and shoved aside to perish by
the highway; but modern moralists have some question
as to whether the destiny of man is inevitably "upward"
(whatever that is), and as to whether the individual who
fails to become a part of the movement is a deliberate
wrong-doer who deserves punishment.

In short, modern psychology, philosophy, psychiatry,
sociology, and ethical thought have left the Enlightenment far behind. But virtually all the colleges and universities, and nine tenths of the professors who administer,
or inflict, the contemporary system of higher education
in America are still marching along in proud lock step
with the Enlightenment. Nobody who knows anything
about the matter can possibly deny this. But I doubt
whether 200 college professors (out of more than 200,000)
in North America have ever thought about it. The typical
American college professor is not inclined to examine
critically the system that has absorbed him.

The notion has got about that the universities are har-

boring an assortment of radicals. One might wish that
there were at least a grain of truth in this notion. But
the fact is that a safe majority of American university
professors vote Republican; a respectable minority are
middle-of-the-road Democrats; and a few are left-wing
Democrats. I myself have never met a professor who was
a Communist, or known anyone who knew one who
was a Communist. Former President of the University of
Chicago, Robert M. Hutchins, who has known far more
professors than I, has had the same experience, or lack of
it. "I have never been able to find a Red professor," he
says. "I have met some who are not wholly satisfied with
present conditions in this country. I have never met one
who hoped to improve them through overthrow of the
government by force." The really typical professor
(though he may sometimes be idealistic and indiscreet
in his utterances) is a moderate conservative in politics,
clothes, and morals. He may permit himself a few little
Mr. Chipsian eccentricities, mostly to get himself talked
about locally; but he seldom ventures outside the conventional fences that confine nearly everybody else in our
society. He is satisfied with the world as well as with
himself.

The Making of a Professor

This brings up the subject of the professor's personality.

Though professors put their students through all manner of personality tests and questionnaires concerning
childhood, sex life, parents, social backgrounds, aptitudes,
attitudes, interests, and so on, there has been (so far as I
can discover) no significant study of the professorial personality. What is said here, therefore, is based not on
statistics, of which there are none, but on more than

thirty years' personal observation of university professors seen at close range.

To understand the university professor, we must look back into his past.

An overwhelming majority of university professors were bookish boys. In elementary school they did not participate, or care to participate, in the rough-and-tumble, highly socialized activities of other boys. They gradually drew apart into a rather lonely world where they found the best society to be themselves, their hobbies, and their books — or, occasionally, one or two other similarly bookish boys. Gradually they developed a feeling of solitariness, of living apart.

Later on, if they attended an especially distinguished high school, where they found their scholastic abilities generally appreciated, they became leaders, with a wondering sense of their own superiority. But, much more probably, they attended the usual type of high school where pretty girls, athletic boys, ROTC officers, and youthful politicians were the school darlings. In such surroundings, the bookish boys retreated still further into themselves and their private world.

Once in college, however, particularly after their freshman year, they suddenly discovered that, in a maturing society, their bookish habits and scholarly attainments were almost universally respected. Here they began to blossom out as appreciated and honored members of society. And here they began to develop the first symptoms of that split personality, a mild but basic schizophrenia, which characterizes so much that is typical of the American university.

As a reaction to the old sense of having been rejected in the lower schools, of having been solitary and unnoticed there, these brilliant university students rebounded to the other extreme: proud of being recognized and acclaimed at last, they developed an acute awareness of their own intellectual superiority. Furthermore, if they were not extraordinarily lucky, they developed an abiding scorn for that old nonintellectual world that had ignored and rejected them so long. Usually this scorn prevented any subsequent understanding of the viewpoints of the nonintellectual, nonbookish world, or even developed into outright hostility toward that world.

The fourth stage was graduate study. On the whole, the life of the graduate student is not enviable. Even if his parents are financially able to support him through graduate school, he feels (with the pride of youth) that he should not be imposing on them. More than likely, therefore, he makes his own way through graduate school with a minimum of aid from his parents. Often he studies under the unhappy circumstance of being supported by a working wife (both he and she being in a continual monthly anguish as to whether she will become pregnant), but more often he studies under some scholarship or fellowship that pays him barely enough to keep alive. All the while he is under extreme intellectual pressure, as well as the essentially undemocratic pressures existing within a university faculty. Having learned to be proud of his own intellect, he now has to develop the habit of deference to professors who have the power of making life miserable for him, or of withholding credits and degrees from him. A wrong move with one of these professors, and his whole career is permanently blighted. As a graduate student, he lives for about four years under these tensions. They leave a permanent mark on him.

Finally, when he becomes a member of the university

faculty, he is still on probation for two or three years. If he cannot favorably impress his superiors, his career is once more jeopardized. And even if he does impress his superiors favorably, even if he does succeed in acquiring tenure at some university, he does not become financially independent and secure for years thereafter — if at all.

The personality that eventually emerges from all this is, typically, underlain with a deep sense of inferiority, fear, and maladjustment, yet overlain by an almost frantic sense of superiority. This deep split in the personality is further complicated by a latent hostility to that which is nonbookish and nonintellectual, and a fluttery insecurity that creates morbid fear of any criticism that may endanger hard-won academic place. Moreover, since only a persistent doggedness of personality could have won through the obstacles that graduate students must overcome, the professor is (by a process of natural selection) a single-minded person without much capacity to view the world impartially, much less appreciatively and lovingly. Finally, if he lands in one of the better universities, he continues to live under tension: he must do research, he must publish, he must play politics, court his superiors, and be sure that he associates with the right people if he hopes for advancement.

Of course, the professor is not unique in having to undergo pressures and tensions; they are common to most careers. If they are mentioned here, it is only to correct the popular concept that the professor lives the placid life of the "retired and uncourtly scholar" or the elegant life of the suave intellectual. Most people do not realize that the professor's personality results from some quite fearful pressures and tensions that have warped, suppressed, or misdirected many an element of character, and made the typical professor at last a quite abnormal personality.

The Professorial Personality

Having worked so painfully and persistently for so many years, some professors think that they have earned a right to lifelong repose thereafter. They become lazy, and never learn anything new, or engage in original research, or do anything more than is required by the minimum needs of their classes. These lazy professors, however, are a minority in the profession. With most professors, the habits of work acquired in early years carry over into later years. Most professors work long and faithfully at tasks that are not inspiring: making out examination questions, writing study outlines, planning laboratory exercises, drawing up reading lists, adjusting schedules, grading papers. Dr. Johnson's definition of a lexicographer fits perfectly the typical university professor: he is "a harmless drudge."

Furthermore, most college professors (having learned to work hard with little recompense) devote a good deal of time, effort, and worry to what they feel is the betterment of the campus community — to endless committee work on entrance requirements and credits and standings of students and scheduling of courses, to conferences with students, conferences on textbook adoptions, conferences on the curriculum, speaking to student groups, speaking to groups outside the university in behalf of better "town and gown" relations — and so on. Though, it must be admitted, this work usually amounts to nothing much but stirring old stew, it is nevertheless done honestly and self-sacrificingly. The university professor seldom responds to the university's plea for help by asking, "What's in it for me?"

But some other professorial qualities are less admirable. I record them here not because I enjoy contemplating them, but because the rest of this book is rather intimately related to those professorial qualities described here.

At least 90 per cent of all university professors are timid men, personally, mentally, and morally. The typical professor is in continual dread of antagonizing, irritating, or disturbing "the administration" — especially if he happens to know that most modern university administrations maintain a secret dossier on each of their professors, and that into this dossier goes every scrap of gossip or criticism that reaches the administration. The professor will go to almost absurd lengths not to appear too often in this dossier, or to endanger his chances of advancement.

Let me give a few examples from my own experience, since no impersonal statistics are available. I have seen famous professors all atremble before going to have a routine interview with the university president; I have seen a professor in a funk because he was wearing a loud sport shirt when he happened to meet the president; I have seen friends by the dozen desert a professor who incurred the displeasure of the administration; I have seen faculty committees pledge themselves to support a certain policy, and have seen most of the members abandon their pledge instantly on finding that the administration opposed the policy; and I remember a startling episode when a professor in open meeting rose and told the President Emeritus: "We can say what we want to now because you have no power over us, and we are no longer afraid of you." Then there was the time, in faculty meeting, when I made some fairly harmless proposal of which, it happened, the administration did not approve. The next day one of my colleagues (a man who is now head of one of the major divisions of one of the most famous old universities in this country) came to the door of my office, looked up and down the hall to see that nobody was watching, plunged inside, quickly closed the door after him, whispered, "I don't see why on earth anybody could have opposed the motion you made in meeting yesterday," and then plunged out the door again.

And there was the other professor, a scientist of international reputation, who complained that, by the new decree from the administration, all orders for material had to be made out in quintuplicate. Standing at the door of his office, he looked up and down the hall, leaned over to peer into the office next door to make sure it was empty, and whispered, "It's a stupid ruling!"

And the other old professor who, when asked to join the thoroughly respectable American Association of University Professors, declared, "I have spent twenty years building myself a place in this department; and I will not risk the administration's disapproval by joining any outside organization."

And the time when an administrative officer, having to entertain a notoriously bloody Latin-American dictator, sent out command-invitations for the faculty and their wives to attend a reception for the dictator. To my knowledge, only one of the ardent "liberals" on the campus stayed away.

This same timidity, inspired by insecurity and long-ingrained habits of humble deference, makes the typical professor one of the readiest of sycophants. I do not mean to say that the professor is any worse in this respect than most people in the business world. The professor is probably better. For the one in twenty professors who would dare hint opposition to a policy supported by the administration, not one in sixty business men could be found to oppose *their* bosses. I am merely saying that it is a mistake for the professors themselves, or for anyone else, to think of the professor as a high-minded, intellectual whose actions and opinions are always influenced by rational and courageous considerations.

At faculty receptions, it is painful to see the eager smiles, the too-quick laughter, the too-assiduous offers of help, the too-obvious attempts to call attention to oneself, as faculty members (and their wives) cluster about those "from whom advancement may befall." One feels that he is watching these insecure people making a play for their livelihoods — or perhaps they are overly ambitious people striving for a place in the little sun of the university campus. It is the same in the official faculty meetings, where the mild jokes of the president and the dean are greeted with as much uproarious laughter as if the faculty themselves were telling jokes to frightened freshmen. This is only human nature, of course; but that is the point. The faculty are only human — all too human.

I know one astute young professor who habitually played chess with the head of his department, invariably let the old man win, and then complimented him on his prowess. (This stratagem paid off handsomely, by the way, with quick advancement.) I know another professor who, as soon as he arrived on the campus from another university, began dogging the footsteps of the chairman of the department, so that one was seldom seen without the other, asking advice on the simplest personal matter from the baby's sore throat to what brand of automobile tires one should buy, laughing at the old man's sallies, serving as a one-man claque when the old man appeared in public, and in general making himself so ridiculous that even the faculty laughed at him. (This stratagem paid off too. Even the most renowned professors are not immune to flattery.)

And there was the professor's wife who (when told of an exceedingly rich townsman's wife coming late to one of the university exercises, and finding no empty seat near the rostrum) cried out indignantly to certain other faculty wives: "If I had seen that Mrs. Blank wanted a seat, I would have given her mine and sat on the ground!" This whole problem, be it said, of the relation of faculty wives to their husbands' advancement waits a Thackeray for adequate delineation. In general, if a wife is pretty, she is expected to play up to the important officials of the university — not in any immoral way, of course, but in a gently coquettish way; and if she is plain, she is expected to become personally involved in the personal problems of the wives of important people. Seldom can a professor become a campus luminary without the expert aid of his wife.

I mention these distressing personal topics here only as an introduction to more strictly professional topics; I have wanted to suggest that the professor has some deeply ingrained limitations of character that he himself ought to recognize, and that the entire nation should be aware of, if higher education is to be improved in America.

The Immovable Object

To turn to less painful, more professional topics, one

would expect that in the intellectual atmosphere of a university campus would be found the most burning desire for intellectual advancement. And indeed it is true that professors are, as a rule, commendably eager to advance, and to welcome advancements, in knowledge. But my experience has been that, in their own personal intellectual attitudes and values, they are as obdurate as granite. At the beginning of their careers, they commit themselves to certain basic systems of value or of behavior, and rarely change thereafter. This obdurateness involves early-adopted literary standards, historical principles, philosophical theories, scientific postulates, personal values. Once a professor has taken his stand in any of these fields, he will, in all likelihood, be found there the rest of his life. The leopard does not change his spots, nor the professor his mind. This is why professors (as a class) so often find themselves caught far out on an intellectual limb when any new great art form, literary method, historical interpretation, philosophical doctrine, or even scientific hypothesis appears. The record of professorial opposition to these advances is long and sad.

This opposition to forward motion (or any motion) extends to the professor's teaching. He early adopts one method of teaching, one method of testing, one method of grading, one opinion of the needs of higher education, one concept of the function of the university, one attitude toward students — and he considers any suggestion that he change to be a personal insult.

Let me give a single rather lengthy example of what I mean. The example is chosen from the mathematics faculty because (one would think) the mathematicians would be logical and impartial if any professors ever are.

I give you my word that every syllable of this example is true, and that the mathematicians who participated in it were well-respected researchers in their profession.

Nearly fifty years ago the mathematical president of a tiny Southern university set up the requirement that all liberal arts freshmen (men and women) should take a stiff course in calculus and analytical geometry. In a recent meeting in which one liberal arts professor tried to persuade the university to drop this requirement, it was pointed out that no other university in the nation required such a course of its liberal arts freshmen.

The Mathematics Professors: That only shows that we are the best university in the nation.

Liberal Arts Professor: Harvard requires no such course; nor does Princeton, nor does Chicago. At Yale, liberal arts students must prove to the mathematics faculty that they are capable of taking such a course before they are even allowed to register in it.

Mathematics Professors: That only proves that we are a better university than Harvard, Princeton, Chicago, and Yale.

Liberal Arts Professor: Neither Oxford nor Cambridge requires it of their liberal arts students.

Mathematics Professors: That only proves that we have the best university in the world.

Liberal Arts Professor: The liberal arts students who have no mathematical aptitudes spend more time on their mathematics than on any other subject, yet they will never use this mathematics afterward, nor is it integrated with any other part of their subsequent education. They could spend their time much better in learning an additional foreign language, or taking additional courses that will help them in their major subjects later on, or in their future careers, or even in taking some mathematics course that would acquaint them with the history and the philosophy of mathematics.

Mathematics Professors: For the very reason that calculus and analytical geometry are hard, they strengthen the minds of those who take the course.

Liberal Arts Professor: But the brain is not a muscle to be strengthened by exercise.

Mathematics Professors: Mathematics gives training in generalized abstract thinking.

Liberal Arts Professor: But in language, literature, history, and art, we spend all our time trying to get our students to be specific and concrete, and to avoid the generalized and abstract.

Mathematics Professors: One learns in mathematics a logical method that helps one in all his thinking.

Liberal Arts Professor: "Transfer of training" is a long-discarded educational theory. It has been proved over and over that the methods used in one field of knowledge can be applied in other fields only rarely and accidentally. The methods in mathematics are useful in mathematics, and not demonstrably useful anywhere else. Being essentially deductive, they are the opposite of methods required in most sciences.

Mathematics Professors: The hard work that students expend on mathematics is good for them; it strengthens their characters; they should learn the necessity for hard work in this world.

Liberal Arts Professor: By the same token, the Mathematics Department should throw away all its calculating machines and electronic devices. If hard work for the sake of hard work is good for people, why doesn't the Mathematics Department practice it?

Mathematics Professors: Knowledge that a stiff mathematical course is required here keeps out all those prospective students who think the university should be a place for idling time away in social activities.

Liberal Arts Professor: It also keeps away the prospective students who are interested in literary, historical, philosophical, and artistic subjects. Besides, when did mathematics become the only difficult course in the university?

Mathematics Professors: The only people who object to the freshman mathematics course in calculus and analytical geometry are those who haven't intelligence enough to pass it.

Liberal Arts Professor: Almost every word you say proves that skill in mathematics and what I should call intelligence have no relation to each other.

In this discussion the most appalling thing was the intellectual obduracy of the mathematics professors. Undoubtedly they could have advanced some excellent arguments for keeping mathematics in the freshman curriculum. But the arguments they did advance were based on intellectual premises adopted decades previously, and not questioned since. This is the mental attitude typical of far the greater part of all university professors, and it explains why the values and methods of the American university have not changed appreciably in at least forty years. Once a position has been adopted by a professor, it is not subject to change, and any question is heresy. Insofar as educational ideals and methods are concerned, the typical professor is much like the typical Bourbon: he never learns anything new or forgets anything old.

Professorial Types

Like all other definitions, the definition of what constitutes a "good professor" must be arbitrary. My own definition would involve the following items, arranged in an ascending order of importance: (1) His students learn well what he teaches them about his subject; (2) his students learn that knowledge and the process of acquiring knowledge are an endless and irresistible source of delight; (3) his students learn to seek, in every circumstance, the best and the highest that lies *within themselves*. By these criteria, hardly one professor in several hundred would receive a grade of A-plus. Not more than one in twenty would receive an A. At least 10 per cent would receive a flat F. Not more than 10 per cent would rate a B. About 30 per cent would deserve a C, and over 40 per cent a D. These estimates are, of course, personal; there are no statistics. But they are based on nearly forty years of interested observation and experience, and they are (if anything) charitable. (I have just asked three of my nonprofessorial friends for their estimates of their former college professors. Without exception, the three rated the professors lower than I have just rated professors in general.)

Essentially, there is only one type of good professor. He is learned, enthusiastic about learning, original, empathic, innately suspicious of rules and regulations that endeavor to uniformize personalities, more eager to encourage students than to judge them, always conscious that appreciation is ten times more efficient as an educational device than is condemnation. This kind of professor has heartened and saved many a student who otherwise would have been lost; and though the other professors do not ordinarily respect him so much as they do their "tougher" colleagues, he is a kind of university conscience whom they cannot forget, whose existence shames them a little, and whose example influences them subtly even though they resist it. His mere presence on the campus is a continuous reminder (disturbing to the administration and to the other professors) that students are, in spite of IBM cards and efficiency-obsessed administrators, individual human beings. It is unfortunate that this professor is so rare on the campus, and a tragedy that he is becoming rarer.

The "bad" professors are much more various. Maybe this fact is vaguely analogous to a remark made by Dorothy Sayers many years ago, "There is only one way to make love, but there are a thousand ways to commit a murder." There is only one way to be a good professor, but there are at least seven ways to be a bad one. Let me describe these seven types of the bad professor:

Worthy of first mention because he may be a very good man while being a very bad professor, is the plain stupid professor. Again, the ways to be stupid are multiple. The stupid professor may be merely ignorant — trying to teach a subject he doesn't know or understand. Or he may be too stupid to know when he is boring people, or when he is antagonizing them, or when he is amusing them at his own expense, or when he is talking over their heads, or when he is insulting their intelligence. Or he may be too stupid to adapt himself to special conditions in the classroom or about the campus, or to elicit the best from the personalities in his classes. Or his stupidity may manifest itself as an intellectual lethargy, or perhaps obduracy, as suggested in the previous section: he does not want to bother to learn anything new, or to revamp his old ideas to make them consistent with current realities. Most commonly, he is a rule-follower because rule-following simplifies life, and he needs to live a simple life.

The second type is the smug professor — the one with a kind of feline complacency and an imperturbable confidence that he is most clever and most knowing. He has proved to himself that he is a pretty smart fellow. For has he not received excellent grades in college, done successful graduate work, written a learned dissertation, received an accolade of various degrees, and enjoyed regular advancements in his position at the university? Has he not published articles in the learned journals? And by diligent research has he not become undisputed master of some small corner of knowledge? Why should he not consider himself rather good?

Besides, he is daily associated with the immature and poorly informed intellects of his students; and the contrast makes him all the more certain, consciously or subconsciously, about his own intellectual pre-eminence. His wife, in order to bolster her own confidence that she herself was pretty sharp in taking him as a husband, plays up to his concept of himself, and trains the children to do the same. I once heard of a professor's small son whose mother had trained him to repeat several times daily: "Papa is a very great man." Under these conditions, how can the professor avoid becoming smug?

As he grows older, the smug professor becomes elegantly conventional, invariably optimistic, critical of just those things that everybody else criticizes. The apotheosis of worldliness, he associates habitually with only the right people (this equals the wealthy families in the town, and the up-and-coming professors on the campus); he participates with voluble enthusiasm in every "cultural" activity that is supported by the right people in the community; he is liberal in his religious and political views, but never so liberal as to offend the right people; he is eager to assist all students who agree with him and admire him; he disapproves of only the crassly independent mind that dares disturb his universe with a question. This type of professor is everywhere evident in every university.

Fortunately less common (but unfortunately still common enough) is the third type of personality produced by the intellectual obduracy characteristic of professors. This is the arrogant professor. He is never arrogant to those "from whom advancement may befall"; but he is arrogant to everybody else — to students, to graduate students, to faculty members who are his inferiors in the campus hierarchy. Most especially, if he hails from the graduate school of some famous university, he is arrogant to the yokel-like students of his new university. All the unhappiness, hostility, and scorn suffered in the graduate student's and the young instructor's soul, while he underwent the insecurities, uncertainties, deprivations, humilities, and drudgeries of his early days, finds release now that the young man has become a professor, now that the subordinate has become a master.

The rudeness of this professor is incredible. He has not the slightest inkling of what Emerson knew so well — that "the secret of education lies in respecting the pupil." He will interrupt students giving oral reports in class by a continual flow of remarks: "That isn't so at all!"; "Oh, no! You've got that all wrong"; "We've had enough of that. Go sit down!" He will cut students down in class with sarcastic remarks. He will write bludgeoning comments on papers. Here are two illustrative incidents that occurred in my presence this very day:

I happen to pause for a moment in a colleague's office. A student comes to the door and says, "Excuse me, Dr. Blank. But did you get that paper on such-and-such a topic that I laid on your desk yesterday?"

"Oh," says Dr. Blank, "so you're the one that wrote that paper? I wondered who on earth could have written one so bad!"

An hour later I am walking across the campus with another colleague. A student in one of my advanced courses stops me for a moment to ask a question. My colleague, who knows the young man, says, "What! Are you taking his advanced course? I thought you were damned lucky to get through my freshman course in the same subject!"

Obviously, professors of this type cannot inspire a student with a desire to learn, or love of a subject, or love of a university that harbors such professors. All the student wants to do is to get out of the university, and shuffle off its unpleasant associations as quickly as possible.

In his extreme form this type of professor has a eunuch-like cruelty. Admittedly, the extreme form is not so frequently found; but just one in a department, or even in an entire college, is the one rotten apple that spoils the whole barrel for the student. This professor specializes in the superior stare, the supercilious tone, the calculated trick of allowing a caller to remain standing, the curt and cleverly ironical answer. He likes to make witty and cutting remarks that set everyone present roaring at the victim's expense; he writes ironical "recommendations" that ruin a young instructor's chances of employment; he asks impossible questions on oral examinations, and then acts as if the candidate were a simple idiot for not knowing the answers. All this builds up his own ego, which requires the constant and morbid sacrifice of others if it is to survive.

A much more common, and much less obnoxious, type is the professor who just does not care about people. He likes science or scholarship, books and libraries; he likes learning, and he may even enjoy talking about what he knows. But he has no real human warmth, friendliness, empathy, or understanding of the personalities and points of view of his students or of his colleagues.

I have seen him, as a mathematics professor, lecture to a class of a hundred students with a pipe in his mouth, his back to the class, and his body hiding the formulae he was writing on the board — formulae which he wrote with his right hand while his left hand followed two feet behind with the eraser. I have seen him, as an English professor, leaning on the lectern, reading lectures in a monotone from an enormous pack of little cards which he picked up one by one. I have seen him, as a biology professor, consider a laboratory exercise as an opportunity for him to do some work of his own, dump materials in the sink or on the tables, and disappear for the next four hours while the students tried to make sense out of the hastily and ambiguously written directions he had scribbled on the board at the last minute, and left with them. I have seen him, as a history professor, reading lectures from a loose-leaf notebook, the lectures consisting entirely of excerpts from the textbook which he had already assigned to the class. I have seen him, as a professor of French literature, plowing right onward in his lecture, never pausing to write name of book or author on the blackboard. I have seen him, as an engineering professor, announce to his class of 50 students at the beginning of the term that, no matter what kind of work any of them did in the course, he was going to give 5 A's, 10 B's, 20 C's, 10 D's, and 5 F's.

The mechanical inhumanness of such professors is quite as likely to repel the student as the smugness and the arrogance mentioned earlier. It attracts him to the subject not at all, inspires him not at all, stimulates in him no desire for learning, or love of his university, or respect for the scholarly-scientific-intellectual ideals for which the university should stand. To be sure, this kind of professor may have something to offer a certain 10 per cent of the undergraduates, or twice that percentage of graduate students. But it is difficult to see how these percentages can be reconciled with the truism, repeated ten thousand times, from Jefferson to yesterday, that education for all the people is a necessity if democracy is to survive. A professor who can educate only one tenth, or even one fifth, of his students is hardly serving the cause of democracy — or hardly returning adequate value for all the tax money that is being spent, and the far greater amount that will be spent in the future, in an effort to educate the young people of America.

Just the opposite of this type of professor is the one (usually young) who tries to "pal around" with his students, be their companion and their equal. A product of early solitude and social rejection, he now overcompensates by trying to make his students like him, not respect him — make them value his friendship, not what he can teach them, make them talk about him among themselves as "a real human being," not as a person who instills in them the desire to learn; make them remember him as an agreeable personality, not as an intellectual influence; make them think of him always as a man whom they like, not as a man who taught them something. Though this professor is far from ideal, three things must be said in his favor. First, he is not a negative element in the university as is the intellectually arrogant professor; second, since young people instinctively imitate those whom they like, he may, if he is a real scholar, inadvertently influence his students to want to learn; and third, as he grows older, feels more secure in the world, does not hunger for friendship as he did in his youth, and acquires the dignity of years, he may possibly become the very highest type of teacher — one who can continually maintain an awareness within himself that he is teaching, not masses of names and faces which have little importance compared with the subject he is teaching, but individual human beings whom he is morally obligated to teach — and teach as well as he possibly can.

The next type of professor, though well known and powerful on the campus, is somewhat difficult to describe. Usually he has produced little in the way of published scholarship or science; he is not particularly interested in research; he is not known as a good, or even popular, teacher. But by means of certain stage properties — such as a tweed suit, a pipe, a rather deep voice, a supercultured accent, knowingness about certain backstairs matters in the history of various great professors and celebrated universities, and a peculiar manner of friendly condescension to everybody, he creates about him an atmosphere of urbanity, civilization, culture. He is just a little cynical, yet he is thoroughly optimistic when you get right down to it; he has no real ideas, yet he gives the impression that he could talk about ideas if it were not so boringly uncivilized to be serious in social intercourse; he scoffs gently at convention, yet co-operates perfectly with every convention that really matters on the campus. The trustees, the president of the university, the heads of departments, and the wealthy people of the town are invariably wild with enthusiasm about him. His complacency assures trustees, president, department heads, and citizens that all is well with the university. Any doubts they may have had are gently swept aside by the mere existence of this worldly and cultured gentleman. Disarmingly frank and humorous in criticizing matters of no consequence, he is all the more comforting when he stoutly defends the essential status quo. An excellent man for lulling and suppressing self-analysis and self-criticism.

The last type of professor to be mentioned here is the one who, working within the new vision of education as the output of an administrative "team," and referring to his immediate superior as "the chief," teaches in a supremely businesslike way, with a team of assistants grading papers, a team of stenographers preparing study aids, a team of secretaries keeping records, a team of aids compiling statistics, and a continual effort by all hands to formulate new student-requirements and educational formulae, and to build up local and state-wide committees charged with this or that educational chore. To this professor-turned-executive, the students are so many items to be processed, so many completed jobs to be turned out according to schedule; education is a business, and the student is both the product and the consumer. Uniformity, efficiency, mass production, and mass consumption are the ideals. Absorbed in this dream, the professor-turned-executive loses sight of the student as a human being, a young person whose welfare is the breath of life to his parents, a separate personality whose uniqueness goes unrecognized in the pursuit of administrative efficiency and teamwork.

Professor versus Professor

In discussing these types of professors as they are related to the work for which they are hired — namely, teaching — I have said little about the professors in relation to themselves. The intradepartmental and interdepartmental bickerings, jealousies, private throat-cuttings, and outright personal treacheries that go on within most universities are incredible to the outsider. It is not true that there are as many cliques in a university faculty as in a girls' school, as much gossip as at a girls' slumber party, as many quarrels over trivialities as at a ladies' aid society, as much protocol as at a diplomatic dinner in Washington, and as much concern about rank as on a naval flagship. But it is almost true. As Professor Lazarsfeld of Columbia University says, "Anyone familiar with the college scene knows that factionalism, backbiting, jealousy and maneuvering for advantage are frequent enough to be an accepted if not inevitable part of academic life." It is not an accident that as a professor becomes older and presumably wiser, he almost invariably withdraws more and more from official association with his colleagues, and becomes a lone wolf. He has learned not to trust his colleagues.

I have known heads of departments who blocked advancement of subordinates out of jealousy because the subordinates were better known than the head, or blocked advancement because a subordinate was, say, of German extraction and the head was French. I have known professors to quarrel bitterly because one ventured to find some minor fault with a pet student of the other, or wanted to count a freshman examination question as worth 30 per cent while the other insisted on only 20 per cent. I have known professors who deliberately exercise their official authority to prevent students from registering in the course of a rival professor; I have known professors to exercise the most profound personal discourtesies to one another simply because of a difference of opinion on some scholarly or scientific matter. And the dreary catalogue could go on and on.

Chaucer long ago expressed the point of all this in a perfect phrase: "The grettest clerks ben not the wisest men." A professor may bear a tremendous burden of learning, but he is still subject to all the common human weaknesses — as well as some uncommon ones peculiar to himself and to his profession. I have thought it worth while to discuss this matter because I wanted to make the following points:

1. College professors are not necessarily good teachers.

2. College professors are not necessarily good men or wise men.

3. College professors do not necessarily know what constitutes sound educational ideals or good educational practice.

4. College professors should realize that they are more than likely to have some grave personality defects, and should try to purge themselves of these defects. It is a moral responsibility to their students and to society for professors to try to perfect themselves as teachers.

5. American colleges and universities as a whole need a stiff dose of self-analysis and self-criticism to purge themselves of the smugness that infects nearly all of them.

6. Students and parents should be less docile in ac-

cepting any kind of professor whom the student happens to draw in the lottery of course assignments, should refuse to be awed by excellent scholarship into thinking that a professor is either a good teacher or an admirable man, should take it upon themselves to find out what constitutes a good teacher, and should demand that every student be treated like a human being instead of like a frankfurter being processed (rather carelessly) in a packing house.

7. If the college professors refuse, or neglect, to try to improve themselves as teachers, or their institutions as instruments for the best possible education of young Americans, the public at large should not hesitate to exert pressure on the universities and the professors. This does not mean that the public at large should decide what and how the universities should teach; only specialists can decide that, and the only specialists in the field are professors in the universities themselves. What it does mean is that the public should continually insist that the universities continually subject themselves to the most rigorous self-examination and the most bitter self-criticism. The somewhat lordly self-satisfaction into which the universities have fallen does not encourage self-improvement. The relation of the public to the university should be somewhat like that of the father of a sick child to the physician. The father should not try to dictate the treatment; but he should insist that the physician attend the child faithfully, read up on the child's disease and the latest approved treatments for it, be acutely alert to the failure of any treatment being attempted, show a willingness to change an ineffective treatment to a new one, exercise diligent self-criticism, and never be satisfied until the child is healthy once again.

CHAPTER FOUR

WHAT THE UNIVERSITIES FAIL TO DO

The Incubus of Puritanism

Because of the influence of early New England on American education and American ideals, a very large element of American culture is still tinged with Puritanism. This Puritan element looms extraordinarily large in the backgrounds and traditions of the American university. Now, whatever else Puritanism may be, it is hardly gay. The Puritan takes life seriously, wants other people to take it seriously, and stands ready to condemn them without mercy if they devote precious time to pleasure, try to enjoy beauty and love and leisure, care more about a well-rounded self-development than a rigorous self-discipline. To this fundamental American Puritanism was added, between the Civil War and the First World War, an eager imitation of British culture, at a time when British culture meant Victorianism, and Victorianism meant "self-reverence, self-knowledge, self-control," and the belief that any man could rise in the world by his own efforts (together with the corresponding belief that any man who did not rise must be lazy, weak, dishonest, or biologically inferior). Methodism and Scotch Presbyterianism can hardly be said to have brought waves of light-hearted gaiety to sweep away Puritan dourness and Victorian seriousness; nor did the severe Lutheranism of hard-working German and Scandinavian immigrants help matters.

To be sure, young America broke with such sobriety in the short decade after the First World War and before the blight of the Great Depression. And America since the Second World War has been bowling along a flowery road of "gracious living" with a delight and an abandon not equaled since the Renaissance in Italy. Most of the age's scientific discoveries have been aimed at making life easier, more pleasant, and more beautiful; and beauty, love, and leisure are demanded with an insistence that would have shocked our Puritan and Victorian ancestors. The spirit of this age is *not,* whatever it may be, Puritan or Victorian. To know this, one has only to look at the Easter-egg-colored automobiles racing in front of one's door, or peep at the bosomy and leggy advertisements in the plush magazines, or note the studied luxuries of the Exurbia to which every American family aspires, or observe the multitude of labor-saving devices ranging from automatic washing machines to electric-eye doors that grace most American homes.

In the midst of a world like this, the university professor continues to insist that his students "work hard," renounce pleasure, anguish over their studies, discipline themselves to the hardships of the scholar's life. With something of the sadism of the Puritan, the typical professor thinks he is neglecting his duty unless he makes life hard for his students; and his colleagues respect him as a teacher only in proportion to his "toughness."

All this is only another example of the typical schizophrenia that mildly bedevils American universities and

American professors. The same professor who insists that his students shall discipline themselves to the hard labor of learning, gets more actual joy out of learning than out of anything else in his life except a few personal affections. He does not go to his books, his desk, his library, or his laboratory "like a quarry-slave scourged to his dungeon"; he goes almost like a lover seeking his mistress. The saddest thing in his life is that each day gives him only sixteen hours in which he can "work." Long ago, in the fine days of the Renaissance, Rabelais understood this joy of the scholar. He set his Gargantua to acquiring an education through observing nature, reading, discussing with others what he had learned and they had learned, practicing the fine arts, engaging in certain handicrafts, receiving training in sports and good manners; and he adds that these activities "soon became so sweet, so easy, and so delightful that it seemed rather the recreation of a king than the study of a scholar."

The failure of the American professor to inculcate the feeling that learning is a delight is one of the saddest weaknesses of the entire system of higher education. Indeed, it is most terribly true that, when a professor mentions in lecture a book which he himself has found delightful, he automatically excludes that book from the voluntary reading of nine tenths of his students. The students reason subconsciously that if the book is education, it must be unpleasant. Not one professor in a hundred does anything to disabuse his students of this tragic misconception by showing them that learning is not a chore but fun, not a renunciation of pleasure but a pursuit of pleasure, not self-sacrifice but self-indulgence. Not only do professors make no effort to convey this feeling about learning, but they make every effort (by personal adjuration and admonition as well as classroom technique) to convey the opposite feeling. It is impossible to attend a faculty meeting concerned with the curriculum without hearing nearly every professor declare that certain courses should be kept in the curriculum for their "disciplinary value," meaning that some courses should be kept just to prove to students that learning must not be thought of as enjoyable.

The American university has become a strange looking-glass world in which plays, poems, and novels originally written for enjoyment become a weary task for students; in which would-be engineers are asked to labor drearily learning how to produce labor-saving devices; in which chemists, draughtsmen, and many other technicians are given *unpleasant* training in the ways and means of making life more *pleasant*. The entire spirit of the universities is at complete variance with the spirit of the age —yet university administrators lie awake at night wondering why 30 to 40 per cent of their freshman students will never graduate, why 10 to 20 per cent of those who remain will be in continuous scholastic difficulty, and why only 10 to 15 per cent of all students are quite satisfactory.

The Impartial Intellect

American intellectuals are constantly deploring the anti-intellectualism of Americans—their hostility to "eggheads," to "brain trusts," to scientific principles having no immediate practical value, to basic research, to scholarly investigation that discredits favorite superstitions, to educators with new ideas about education, to thinkers who question popular mores. The intellectuals (most of whom are university professors) who do all this deploring have themselves (and their counterparts in the public schools) to thank for this widespread hostility toward intellectualism.

The ideal of the university professor and of the whole university system is to be impartial, objective, impersonal, purely intellectual. At the same time, something of the old Hebraic-Puritanical spirit of righteous and rigorous judgment prevails. *"Mene, mene, tekel, upharsin"*: Thou art weighed in the balances, and art found wanting. "And they were judged out of those things which were written in the books, according to their works . . . every man according to their works." Weeping and wailing and gnashing of teeth avail nothing against the inexorable and impartial and impersonal law. I have heard professors, presumably acting *in loco dei*, declare: "If a student's average in my course is 60, he gets a D; if it is 59.9, he gets an F." I have heard professors say, "I try not to know my students personally; if I get to know them, I will get to sympathizing with them and with their point of view, and will not be able to grade them justly." I have known cases in which a student lost a father or a mother during the final examination period, or was sick during the examination, or even had broken an arm the day before the examination—yet, youthfully foolhardy, insisted on taking the final examination—and failed. Whereupon the committee in charge of such matters announced: "If we are going to have rules, we should follow them. We cannot start a precedent by making personal exceptions." I have repeatedly seen committees finish a student's college career because he failed by two per cent in a "required" course, though all the rest of his grades were A's and B's. I have seen students denied a valuable scholarship because they were automatically given a failing grade on a term-paper handed in two days late, though there was a good excuse, and the professor himself was the most notoriously dilatory and tardy man on the faculty.

All this comes from the professor's feeling that his main duty is not to teach, but to be an impartial and impersonal judge, and that the chief business of the student is to make grades, not learn to love learning. Professor C. Page Smith, of the History Department, U.C.L.A., has recently written on this aspect of university education. His article is so sound and so pertinent that I quote from it at length:

> I suspect that largely as a result of the grading system a majority of the students regard the professor as, in a sense, the enemy. That is to say, the professor represents an unknown quantity that has potentiality of damaging the student. As professor he is in a position of almost unlimited power. To counter this the student has a kind of cunning which he has acquired as a by-product of the educational process . . . He knows that if, like the psychologist's pigeon, he pecks the right button, he will get a kernel of corn . . .
>
> The teacher is, of course, as much a victim of our testing conventions as any student. The examinations play an important part in his conception of himself as teacher and scholar. Not infrequently he comes to view them as weapons in a contest between himself and his students . . .
>
> By the time they are upper classmen, the majority of students are thoroughly conditioned to the corruption of marks, and it is correspondingly difficult to break through to the individual, to lure him into any free and uninhibited expression of feeling or opinion . . . The student accepts the system because it can be figured out, anticipated, and made, in general, to

yield the desired token. The professor often values it for its very impartiality and 'objectivity.'

Almost all professors require students to hand back copies of examination questions; some professors forbid advanced students to hold review sessions for freshman courses; all professors participate in an elaborate game of mystery and secrecy about examination questions. They forget that the student should be helped to learn by any means that seems to work: learning, not examinations and grades, is the ideal. It would seem that if the student could pass all the professor's examinations for the last few years, the student would have learned a good deal; and perhaps one of the most effective ways of getting the student to learn answers to questions would be to tell the student beforehand what the questions are to be. Again one notes the typical professorial schizophrenia—a confusion between teaching and grading, and a desire to have the student learn answers to presumably important questions, yet an almost morbid fear that the student will find out what the important questions are. It is a confusion that results from a last-century's concept of impersonal and impartial intellectuality, intermingled with the Puritan itch for measuring personal worth by reference to certain arbitrarily fixed standards and commandments.

It is not surprising that a student subjected to four years of this sort of treatment carries away from the university a well-developed suspicion of university professors latent hostility to the intellectual system which they represent, and conviction that the normal professor-student relationship is that of contestants trying to outmaneuver each other.

(Perhaps it is worth remarking that, if impartial and impersonal intellect constituted the realities, or even the

desirabilities, of human life, the professors might be justified in insisting on it. But the psychologists in the universities themselves never cease reiterating that man does
not exist by intellect alone—that, indeed, pure intellect
constitutes only a tiny and derivative fraction of human
personality. Below the level of intellect, the psychologists
patiently repeat, there lies the vast world of the subcon-
scious and the unconscious—of emotion, feeling, inhibi-
tion, compulsion, instinct; fear, desire, love, prejudice,
hate; the complex imprint of pressures from society, home,
school, friends; and the influence of the economic, political, international, and military stresses of all the years
during which the student has lived. Trying to cultivate
this complex personality in the simple terms of intellect,
as the universities do, is as unrealistic as would be the
attempt to make an automobile run efficiently by assidu-
ous painting, waxing, and polishing of the body. It is
another symptom of our educational schizophrenia that
we all realize this, yet we construct an educational system
that, in the upper grades of high school and in practically
all college courses, acts as if the human personality con-
sisted of intellect alone.)

Nothing Original, Please

It is generally assumed in universities that the students
must fit precisely into the system by which the university
functions. The student is made for the system, not the
system for the student. It is expected of the student that
he cease to be a unique personality, and become a part
of the "unified democratic community," a cog, a robot
running mechanically along the grooves of system. The
student who tries to escape from the grooves, in however
limited a manner, is always astonished (on his first at-

tempt at this sort of thing) at the opposition he meets. The student whose native language is German cannot take third-year German because the rules of the system say that first-year and second-year German are prerequisites to third-year German. The student who has avidly read poetry all his life, written poetry, and published poetry cannot take a course in modern American poetry because it is a junior course and he is only a sophomore. The engineer who wants to take a course in the history of philosophy all but incites a riot among the engineering professors. The physical education major who wants to take an advanced course in writing is told that his schedule forbids it. The student who registers for a course, visits it three times, finds it is not what he thought it was, and asks to be transferred to another course must pay a stiff fee: the point is that it is far better for the student to be saddled for a year with a course he doesn't want, and for the instructor to be saddled for a year with a student he doesn't want, than for the system to be broken and trouble caused in the registrar's office. "We are faced," says Bertrand Russell, "with the paradoxical fact that education has become one of the chief obstacles to intelligence and freedom of thought."

After encountering the astonished gaze of professors and administrators a few times, and being told with an air of patient tolerance that his unorthodox proposal is quite impossible, the brash student gives up. He must fit into the system, or perish.

In the classroom, conformity is even more necessary; any deviation may prove fatal. The student who steps out of the groove will be withered with professorial sarcasm, or given a bad grade, or denied a recommendation. If he has a questioning personality, he must suppress it (except with a very few professors) and echo back what he has been told. Even if he is phenomenally gifted in one field (such as writing, art, music, mathematics, or biology) he is never officially recognized as a unique person—that would be highly irregular and would set a precedent—but must take a flock of "required" courses that only chafe and thwart him. If he has any original ideas or criticisms, he must have them within the prescribed intellectual limits, and must not expect to enjoy youth's privilege of being allowed to be wrong. I have known professors to grow furious at a student for suggesting that "Lycidas" is a boresome poem (which it is), or for doubting the professor's interpretation of the symbolism in *Moby Dick*, or for saying that Shakespeare's plays contain a large element of melodrama. I have also known any number of students who, having questioned or doubted, and having been withered by the professor, have sworn solemnly, "I'll never open my mouth again in that course if I have to take it a hundred years."

Former President of the University of Chicago, Robert M. Hutchins, has said: "It must be remembered that the purpose of education is not to fill the minds of students with facts; it is not to reform them, or amuse them, or make them expert technicians in any field. It is to teach them to think." Practically any professor in any subject will echo this sentiment. A thousand times I have heard professors declare, "I don't like students who merely remember; I want students who will THINK." But I have never heard any professor, who insists on students *thinking*, say precisely what he means by *thinking*. When you press the professor for an answer, you find that he always means that the student should *think* just what the professor *thinks*, come to the same conclusions that the professor has reached, and hold the same values in philosophy, literature, science, and art that the professor has. Let any student do a little *thinking* to the contrary, and the professor will tell him, "You are just not *thinking!*"

As for "merely remembering," or actually memorizing, let any student try to get along without it, and the chances are 49 to 1 that he will be rewarded with an F in the course. On the other hand, if he has a good memory, or if he is willing to spend the necessary time to memorize, the chances are 49 to 1 that he will make no less than a B in the course.

Creative thinking and achievement are seldom encouraged in the universities, and are often actually discouraged. In justice, however, let me hasten to say that departments of art and architecture in the modern university do often set a high value on original creativeness; and English and music departments make a gesture in that direction. But the departments in which far the greater number of students major have no place for the original and creative undergraduate. Even English departments and music departments are not eager to recognize and encourage the creative student. In the current catalogue of one of the large state universities, chosen at random, the English department lists 75 courses, of which only two are in creative writing. In the same catalogue, the music department lists 235 courses, of which only four are in original musical composition. As in George Moore's day, it is still true that college education is likely to "prove fatal to anyone with a spark of artistic feeling."

As a general rule, creative ability is discouraged. It is thought of as a distraction from scholarship, or as a lazy student's delightful refuge from the hard "discipline" of learning, or as a suspiciously rebellious gesture of individualism in the midst of a right and comfortable system, or as a subterfuge of the uniquely endowed student to escape the tedium of "required" courses. Just yesterday a young graduate student in history came to me and asked about the university's student Writers' Club. As an undergraduate, he had won several major prizes in poetry. I invited the young man to come around and visit the club.

"Not me!" said the young man, laughing. "If I went I'd have to go in a false beard and under an assumed name to keep Dr. Blank [his graduate adviser] from finding out!"

At the end of every year, when examinations arc all done and grades are all in, many students come to me with poems, plays, and stories to criticize, and say that they have not ventured till then to make public their creative interests. They are quite right; creative activity is only grudgingly permitted in the universities.

Is Knowledge Enough?

Perhaps the universities ought to be concerned with nothing but impartial and impersonal intellectuality. Some apologists have felt so. But there are several reasons why some other people have felt that the objective of pure intellectuality is not altogether enough. For one thing, as I have already said, it is virtually impossible to separate pure intellectuality from personality except in a very few of the sciences. In economics, history, literature, art, music, architecture, philosophy, religion, law, government, sociology, business administration, and in many aspects of geology, biology, paleontology, and even physics and chemistry, getting rid of the strictly personal element is forever impossible. For another thing, it is probable that society, which foots the gigantic bill for most education, will always demand more for its money than remote intellectuality unrelated to society's needs and ideals. Finally, impersonal and impartial intellectuality may lead into some dangerous nightmare zone where love, compassion, human feeling, and morality may be frozen to death. It is hard to forget that, before the Second World War, the German people were the most literate and the best educated in all Europe, and that German scientists had won more Nobel prizes than all the rest of the world's scientists put together—yet the German people acquiesced with good grace in the enormous immoralities of the Hitler government. Anyone who remembers these facts about recent German history can hardly acquiesce in the belief that "the universities ought to be concerned with nothing but impartial and impersonal intellectuality."

Yet, in far the greater part of its activities, the university, obsessed with the fundamentally unrealistic ideal of "impartial and impersonal intellectuality," does practically nothing to insure that the student shall feel a moral responsibility to use his intellectual achievements for the good of the community, the nation, and the human race. On the contrary, the university is largely concerned with teaching the student a profession by which he can become financially successful as an individual without reference to the rest of mankind. Whatever sense of moral responsibility the student may eventually acquire, he does not get it from the university.

Nor does the university, concerned as it is with matters of "impartial and impersonal intellect"; that is, with historical facts, scholarly facts, scientific facts, natural laws, and research to discover more of these facts and more of these laws, seek to develop in its students certain attitudes that seem vastly important to the welfare of mankind, but can hardly be called "impartial and impersonal intellect." Some of these attitudes involve a receptivity to *all* facts, not just the ones that are the subject of today's research problem, facts that are unpleasant, shocking, discomforting, hostile to old beliefs, as well as those that are pleasant, soothing, comforting, and friendly to old beliefs. Or it may be an attitude of open-mindedness; that is, a willingness to try to understand why other people think and act as they do, without necessarily thinking and acting in the same way oneself. Or it may be intellectual and spiritual honesty and courage in the face of the popular and the fashionable. Or it may be a humbly democratic attitude instead of the proud and snobbish attitude that so many of the well-to-do and the well-educated adopt toward the poor and the uneducated. Or it may be a stubborn self-respect that refuses to make dishonest concessions, in the form of flattery, obsequiousness, and fawning obedience, for the sake of personal gain. Or it may be certain ideals and standards of conduct that will not be sacrificed for the expedient and the profitable. Or it may be a sense of obligation to society, resulting in service to society, in payment for what society has contributed to one's own welfare. Or it may be such concern for the welfare of mankind as leads to perfect agreement with Donne's famous and wonderful statement: "No man is an island entire of itself; every man is a piece of the continent. . . . Any man's death diminishes me, because I am involved in mankind"—and not only any man's death, but the suffering, the ignorance, the unrealized selfhood, the stunted personality, the poverty, and the oppression of any man, woman, or child anywhere on this planet. These are some of the attitudes that the universities, in their attempt to educate the younger generation, might try to cultivate. Nor can they shirk their responsibility by saying that their province is the cold intellect alone. Intellect is not an island entire by itself; it is a piece of a continent. The universities cannot do less than take all that continent for their province.

But even in the limited area of mere intellect, it is doubtful whether the universities do a good job of educating even that 10 to 15 per cent of undergraduates whom they regard as successful. The universities are much more inclined to cultivate a *knowing* mind than a *questioning*, a *questing* mind. Yet the *thinking* that the professors are forever hoping to find among their students is born in a question and spends its life in a quest. The typical professor practices intellectual birth-control by discouraging questions in the undergraduate, and demanding only that the undergraduate, like a small bird, receive what is put into him, and regurgitate it on demand.

Because the universities have failed, for most of their students, in all these matters, one can find the greatest physical scientists holding to the most elementary and primitive religious beliefs, the greatest physicians opposing all proposals that will improve the health and lengthen the life of the people but will cut into the physicians' personal incomes, the most successful engineers supporting all sorts of false theories about race, graduates of the most famous women's colleges becoming isolationists and segregationists, well-educated industrial leaders everywhere regarding laboring people as only units of production, and most college graduates unaffected in their childhood religious and political faiths by anything they learned in four years at the university.

I still remember the shock I had when, as an undergraduate, I heard how cruelly and arrogantly the college president berated an old janitor for some insignificant carelessness; and when I learned what starvation wages the university paid its janitors; and when I found that the philosophy professor lacked the courage to commit himself one way or the other on the matter of the Virgin Birth; and when the logics professor explained why he sat in the fashionable dress circle at the symphony instead of the balcony where the music could really be heard better ("I have to get up very early in the morning, and it delays my getting home just that much longer when I have to walk all the way down from the balcony"); and when I learned that the outstanding mathematician on the campus belonged to one of the most primitive and fundamentalist religious sects; and when a great professor (later a college president) spent two hours personally attacking, in class, a senior who had written for the student newspaper a semihumorous article questioning the value of the education he had been receiving in the past four years. It began to dawn on me in those days that higher education lacked something that I thought was essential. In the thirty-five years that have followed, that early opinion has been not only confirmed, but intensified.

CHAPTER FIVE

HOW BADLY CAN YOU TEACH?

Professorial Buck-passing

It is an old army game for college professors to hold grave conferences and make dire public announcements on the inferior quality of the modern high school graduate; for the high school teachers to be scandalized by the poor quality of the junior high school graduates; for the junior high school teachers to speculate about what is going to happen to the world if the elementary school teachers continue training children so poorly; for the elementary school teachers to blame all their classroom troubles on uncooperative parents; and for parents to write letters to the papers, and besiege school boards, and hold councils of war, all intended to turn the responsibility back to the teachers and the school system and the curriculum and the methods of instruction.

As a commentary on the constant professorial lament that the poor training of the modern high school student is responsible for the poor scholastic showing of the modern college student, I should like to make five short observations:

First, no freshman ever knows as much as he should—

neither does any sophomore, any junior, any senior, any graduate student, or any professor. If the freshman already knew all he ought to know, there would be no need for him to come to college. It is precisely for the reason that he does not know as much as he ought to know that his parents send him to college, and society is glad to have him there.

Second, it is my impression that the high schools are doing at least as good a job now as they ever did, and in most cases they are doing a better job. In thirty years of university teaching I have noticed a steady improvement in the basic cultural attainment of most students. This improvement may be due to the fact that more and more high schools are dividing their courses of instruction into two groups, one for students intending to go to college, and the other for students not intending to go to college. Thus the colleges have to deal with only a pre-selected group, which has been specifically prepared for college work.

Third, whether or not the high schools are doing a good job, it is the business of the college professor to take whatever material the gods send him, and teach it. If the material happens to be bad, then the business of the professor may be a little more difficult. But that is all the more reason why he should look to his competence as a teacher. He is certainly not benefiting the nation by throwing out 40 per cent of the students who come to him, and refusing to give them any kind of "higher" education.

Fourth, so-called poor high school preparation does not necessarily make a poor college student. When I was a very young man I taught in colleges in one of the most backward of the Southern states. The colleges were compelled by law to admit any student who could show a diploma from any high school in the state — at a time when this state contained some of the most underprivileged schools in the nation. I found that about 10 to 15 per cent of these students were completely out of place in college. But the others were as responsible and responsive, as eager to learn, and as capable of learning as any students I have had since. It just happens that the alumnus of my own university who has become the science professor of whom the university is most proud, a man of worldwide reputation, came from a little nonaccredited high school in which several of the teachers did not even have the B.A. degree.

Finally, if a student has learned to write reasonably "correct" English, and to read English with a fair measure of understanding, he needs no further preparation for the university—unless he happens to be planning a career in science, in which case he will need mathematics through algebra and plane geometry. Practically all college courses except English and some of the science courses are taught at the beginner's level; and even some of the science courses (biology, geology, and psychology, for example) require no previous preparation in high school. If a student can read English and write English well, he is prepared for college. Too often those professors who complain that their freshmen are "unprepared" are merely trying to rationalize their own failure.

Student Reading versus Professorial Writing

At this point I wish to digress for a moment to speak of a very special complaint that professors are forever making about their freshmen. Not being able to prove that high school graduates are unprepared in specific ways for college work, the professors have settled on *poor reading ability* as one major defect that seems ubiquitous. They have made "reading ability" the mainstay of their complaints, as well as of their entrance examinations.

The professors are on safe ground here. For one thing, it is quite possible that young people today, accustomed to visual and auditory education through television, cinema, and radio, cannot absorb the printed page as well as their grandfathers did. But I have never seen any actual evidence to prove that this is so. And even if it is so, "Other gifts have followed, for these, I would believe, abundant recompense." The modern high school graduate knows more about music, drama, geography, politics, recent history, science, mechanics, and adjustment to society for the sake of a happy and socially useful life than his grandfather ever did. Moreover, even if it should be true that the modern youth is more responsive to visual and auditory education than to literary education, we need not be too alarmed. When, several centuries ago, youth in the Western world ceased memorizing lessons and reciting them by rote, and began to depend more and more on the printed word, I am sure that the professors of the day felt that education was being debased. Some modern educators undoubtedly feel the same way when they suspect that the old reading instrument is being replaced by the new visual and auditory instruments. But that groping, inquisitive, prying, discontented temperament that has brought the human species this far is not likely to fail man now; whatever instrument best helps him satisfy his insatiable curiosity, he will use. The professors need not worry; if the human animal becomes extinct, it will not be through intellectual lethargy, but its opposite.

Another reason why it is possible for professors to

demonstrate the inability of modern students to read properly is that it is virtually impossible for any writer to say any but the simplest things in English, and hope to be understood. If any ten professors can read any fairly abstract or complex passage in English, and derive exactly the same meaning out of it, they have performed a miracle. Yet each one of these same professors expects his students to derive exactly the same meaning from their reading that he would derive. If they fail to derive his meaning, he announces far and wide that the modern student cannot read.

Absolutely at random I open the number of the *Journal of Higher Education* (a strictly professorial project) that happens to be lying on my desk, and find this sentence at the beginning of an article by Dean Herbert Stroup of Brooklyn College:

> The two most commonly advocated aims of student activities are overly familiar: the development of the personal maturity of the individual student, and the growth of democratic citizenship responsibility on the part of the students.

Almost every word of it is ambiguous, and capable of misinterpretation. One has only to ask just who it is that has *aimed* and *advocated;* and what "commonly" means; and what "student activities" the author is talking about (love-making, studying, eating, playing tennis, or what?); and who is "overly familiar" with these "aims" (I, for one, never heard of them till this moment); and exactly what the phrases "personal maturity" and "democratic citizenship responsibility" mean; and who is to determine what is "growth" and what is degeneration—in order to see how easy it would be for a dozen different students to get a dozen different meanings out of this sentence . . . and then be accused of not knowing how to read. This is not hair-splitting; it is an intensely serious matter. Three students asked to paraphrase the first phrases of this sentence might say:

> The two most commonly advocated aims of the college program of studies . . .
> The two most commonly advocated aims of student social affairs on the campus . . .
> The two most commonly advocated aims of the intramural athletic program . . .

Three other students asked to paraphrase "personal maturity" might substitute the phrase "the ability to assume the financial responsibility of a family," or "the ability to get along with other people without being selfishly demanding," or "the stable relationship of a person toward God." Who could say that any of these students did not know how to read? Yet how many of these six different interpretations (together with their many permutations and combinations, and other interpretations of still other phrases in the sentence) would be counted right in the scoring if this sentence appeared on a college entrance examination? And who can say that just such a sentence would not appear on an examination? After all, did not a college professor and a dean write it?

If it should seem that this sentence is accidentally ambiguous, here are the last sentences of the same article:

> It is clear that there are strengths and weaknesses in all the intentions as theoretical means of understanding student activities; some combination would enhance the final truth of the matter. Further study, bolstered by empirical investigation, is required to establish the validity of such constructs and to determine their mode in concrete situations.

I myself would be at a complete loss if I were asked to tell what these sentences mean; and doubtless most young high school graduates would be little better off.

If it still seems that the article is accidentally ambiguous, here are the first few and the last few sentences of the very next article (also written by a professor who might be grading students on their ability to read) in the same number of the *Journal of Higher Education*. All the sentences are studded thick with words, phrases, and ideas so vague that the meanings they bear must vary enormously with every individual reader who carefully considers them:

> The college of liberal arts utilizes many educational agencies to achieve its aims. The emphasis placed upon extra-classroom activities depends upon the philosophy of education which predominates in a particular college. The use of the term "extra-classroom" involves a point of view in respect to the breadth and inclusiveness of the curriculum.
>
> Curtailment of liberal education to the point of neutralization will be deplorable and shortsighted educational statesmanship. Any intelligent reorganization of the resources of the college of liberal arts demands a proper evaluation and adequate utilization of extra-classroom activities.

Even when English is used at the kindergarten stage of simplicity, it can seldom be pinned down to exact and unambiguous meanings which anybody can "read" to the complete satisfaction of everybody else. If I say to a small child, "Drink your milk," I am expecting him to interpret the command in a far more precise way than I may be justified in doing. The child may set his cup on the floor, and lap up the milk as he has seen his puppy doing; or he may dip it up with his cupped hand; or he may soak his napkin in it, and then suck the napkin. He is, in all these cases, following my command; he is drinking his milk. Not being a mind reader, how could he tell that when I said, "Drink your milk," I actually meant to say, "Raise the edge of your cup to your mouth, open your mouth slightly, insert the edge of your cup into the slightly opened mouth, tilt the cup just a little, pour a small quantity of milk into your mouth, swallow that milk, then tilt the cup a little more, and repeat the process till the cup is empty." Sometimes those professors who grade students on their "abiltity to read" expect the students to be, not readers, but mind readers.

But it is not only the language itself that prevents accurate reading; it is the language as used in the textbooks, essays, articles, study-sheets, and instructions that the professors write, and expect their students to "read." Not one third of the professors who complain so bitterly about the inability of their students to read well can write precisely and intelligibly, or express themselves precisely and intelligibly in lectures, or ask precise and intelligible examination questions. In printed books by acquaintances of mine, I have seen expressions like "The substance divides into two unequal halves"; I have seen laboratory directions instructing students to "Draw a square about twice as long as broad"; I have seen examination questions asking students to "Discuss the use of various technical devices in *Huckleberry Finn*"; I have heard lectures crammed with sentences like "The idea of history, philosophically reinterpreted, may well serve to express the value aspect of unfolding significance of reality as we know it especially in human activities"; I have seen psychological tests which asked the subject to fill the blank in the sentence, "4 is to 8 as 8 is to ——," where any answer but "12" was counted wrong; I have graded papers (my own and other professors') in which every student in the class had the identical wrong answer, making it perfectly apparent that the instructor had failed to make himself clear on the matter involved. Yet professors are gravely concerned because "Our students just can't read."

Reading is always a relative matter — relative to what certain words mean and imply to the writer and what they mean and imply to the reader; relative to the personal backgrounds of the writer and the sometimes very different personal backgrounds of the reader; to the educational backgrounds of the writer and the sometimes very different educational backgrounds of the reader; to the philosophical outlook (theological, political, economic, etc.) of the writer and the sometimes very different philosophical outlook of the reader. A good many professors of English would have difficulty reading a textbook on nuclear physics to the satisfaction of any physicist; and a good many physicists would have difficulty reading a textbook of prosody to the satisfaction of any English professor. But these technical difficulties are among the least: it is the personal experiences and differences in background that make accurate reading so rare. Thus "liberal" and "conservative" carry very different meanings, emotions, and implications to different Americans; "democratic" is a word of praise in both America and Russia, but it bears contradictory meanings to Americans and to Russians; "God" is one thing to a Roman Catholic priest, and a very different thing to a well-educated Hindu; some Americans would interpret "segregation" as an unmitigated evil, some as an unmitigated blessing, and a sentence like "Ending racial segregation in America will have profound effects on the nation as a whole" might be paraphrased by one student, "Ending racial segregation in America will create grave dangers for the country as a whole," and by another student, "Ending racial segregation in America will benefit the entire nation."

Much of the time the professorial complaint that "Our students just can't read" amounts actually to one of two things: first, that "Many professors and other academicians just can't write"; or second, that "The experiences and thought patterns of the students are just not uniform with those of the professors." Most professors in most universities find it quite disturbing to encounter a student whose mind is not attired in the same uniform as the professors'.

All this does not mean that every student who graduates from high school "knows how to read." Far from it! Undoubtedly the high schools are giving their students less and less practice in reading. Nevertheless, the professorial excuse that "Our students just can't read" is too often assigned as a cover-up for professorial lack of empathy, imagination, power of clear self-expression, judgment in choosing well-written material for the student to read, and (above all) ability to awaken the student's interest in the reading material.

How to Teach Freshmen Badly

Once the prospective freshman has convinced the authorities that he "knows how to read," and has been admitted to the university, and has got his courses arranged to the satisfaction of the curriculum people, he starts attending classes.

It is not the least of the sins of the universities that many of the basic courses in the all-important freshman year (just when the student is establishing fundamental values and attitudes about learning) are taught by young graduate students. These young teachers lack experience, and have usually had little counsel on the methods or the ideals that a university teacher should have, no real indication from older faculty members that good teaching is an important goal, and no great incentive (and very little time) to do anything well except try to make A's in their own courses and write acceptable dissertations. In English, foreign languages, and mathematics, this condition prevails almost universally; it is not so common in the sciences, in history, and in economics, but in even these courses a large amount of instruction is done by young undergraduate and graduate assistants who have had little experience and no training in the art of teaching. Just last week the Dean of Sciences of a university with almost 20,000 students told me: "When we hire young fellows and assistants, we ask ourselves only one question: Is the young man capable of going ahead and doing good research as a graduate student? We don't give a damn about his teaching ability. We let the students sink or swim; it's their affair, not ours."

Though few deans and departmental heads are quite that blunt about the matter, I know of no dean or departmental head in any university who, when the chips are in, actually feels or behaves any differently. As a result, the freshman, right when the pattern of his entire experience of higher education is being set, is guided and dominated in much of his basic college work by untrained young instructors whom nobody expects to be good teachers. What is more, these young instructors are otherwise occupied in matters that the entire university considers far more important than teaching; they are often abominably conceited; they have no concept about what higher education is for in relation to the individual and to society, and no understanding of human nature; they are only half-informed in the subject that they pretend to be teaching; and they usually hide their ignorance and inexperience with a callow cynicism and a hard-boiled cruelty that is appalling.

This is no exaggeration. It is the usual world of the freshman, the one that gives him his first impressions of university life, and that establishes most of his fundamental attitudes toward higher education for the rest of his university career. That university faculties should treat their freshmen like this, and still lament that it is only the very rare and occasional freshman who develops a love of his subject, an interest in learning, an enthusiasm for intellectual experience, a delight in the entire university atmosphere, is one of the best illustrations of inconsistency and of the almost criminal negligence of most universities.

How to Teach Upper-Classmen Badly

In the postfreshman years the student has more experienced, but not necessarily better, teachers. Reasons for the lack of improvement are, principally, five.

First, it is rare to find any teacher who has not succumbed, mentally and temperamentally, to the pressures of the system in the matter of examinations, grades, and credits. The ideal he holds up to himself is to teach "a good stiff course"; and the ideal he holds up to his students is to make good grades on the examinations, and get credit for the course. He does not try to make his students understand how there can be pleasure in learning; he does not try to lead them to want to learn more and more all their lives; he does not try to show them how questions and problems lie lurking dangerously at the very fountainhead of the knowledge he is trying to impart. Among the academic courses, only a few (10 to 20 per cent) make any attempt to link the student's learning with the pressing intellectual, artistic, political, social, moral, and religious problems that he must face daily; among the science courses the percentage is still smaller. The professor makes the grade the thing. The student learns his facts and his scientific processes, gets his grade, wins his credit, graduates, and thereafter applies his education to no problem except that of making money. And the professor doesn't care.

A second reason why teachers of the upper classes are seldom good teachers, no matter how experienced they may be, is that they have somehow got the notion that "upholding the standards of the university" means essentially giving many low grades. This is a fallacy deeply ingrained in every university that I know anything about, and in almost every professor. Again and again I have heard professors mention the high percentage of bad grades among students majoring in their departments, and the low percentage of students who finally manage to get degrees from their departments. When questioned, they say with obvious pride, "I am doing what I can to uphold the standards of the university." Again and again I have seen lifted eyebrows and significant glances when some professor confessed that nobody failed in one of his courses. I have heard chairmen of committees sit down to go over grades of students at term's end, and say, "Let's see how many of the bastards we can get rid of." I can remember that, even when I was a student, I heard a member of the administration sneering about the greatest professor and the most inspiring man I ever knew: "The old fool never fails anybody in his courses!" There is no doubt that a large number of professors think that their success as teachers depends directly on the number of bad grades their students make. If any professor gives enough bad grades, he will soon get a reputation with the university administration, with his colleagues, and throughout the graduate school as being one of the ablest and sharpest members of the faculty. It is no joke that if a young professor just arrived on the campus wishes to establish himself solidly, he has only to start giving many bad grades, and talking earnestly and in public about "upholding the standards of the university."

A third reason why professors are likely to be bad teachers I have already mentioned in another connection. It is the idea (maintained in spite of their own personal experience to the contrary) that learning is unpleasant *work*. "The world feels," says Jacques Barzun, "that drudgery, discipline, and conformity are the social virtues par excellence" — and the educational virtues, too. It is plain to most professors that, unless a student expends blood, sweat, and tears, he is not getting an education. This is a relic of the Hebraism (Puritanism and Victorianism) that Matthew Arnold criticized. In some ways, Whitehead's book on education is a vessel of this old tradition: "The essence of education is that it be religious . . . A religious education inculcates duty and reverence." In strong contrast is Plato: "Do not train boys to learning by force and harshness, but lead them by what amuses them." It is a fearful comment on the university classroom that 80 to 90 per cent of the students undoubtedly regard it as a boring necessity, a dull adjunct to those really exciting portions of university life, the dances, the athletic contests, the sororities and fraternities and clubs, the social functions. If one questions the percentages hazarded here, one has only to listen to the cheers that go up when a professor announces that the class will not meet next time, and the boos when it is announced that some scheduled dance or athletic meet has been arbitrarily cancelled.

The typical professor accepts this situation with resigned stoicism, just as he accepts age and sickness, and takes refuge from it in his own researches. It does not occur to him to try to make his classes as fascinating as a basketball game, or as pleasant as playing bridge in the student lounge. Indeed, the bitter truth is that, if he does try to make his students like his classes, his colleagues look askance at him as a "popularizer." He must be dull and hard if, in professorial eyes, he is to be great. Not one professor in fifty can understand that the process of learning can be, and should be, in Milton's words, "so sweet, so green, so full of goodly prospects, and melodious sounds on every side, that the harp of Orpheus were not more charming." Instead, professors (and university administrations) believe that the student seeking an education must expect none of those "refined and delicate pleasures that spring from research and education," but only toil, trouble, pain, and tedium. If the student is not able to pay this price, then he is a shallowpate; and if the professor does not demand it, he is a "popularizer."

A fourth reason for bad teaching is mere negligence or indifference on the part of the professor. He may simply not try to be a good teacher. This attitude may arise from any one or more of several causes. The professor may be lazy; he may not want to stir himself sufficiently to teach well. Or he may be so interested in his own researches in library and laboratory that he considers teaching a distraction to which he gives as little time and thought as possible. Or he may be extremely ambitious for advancement, and, knowing that advancement in all major universities depends upon frequent publication rather than good teaching, he may deliberately (and selfishly) pare down to a minimum the time he gives to his classes. Or he may have outside interests that keep him too busy to be a good teacher — part-time jobs in business or industry, his own investments, do-it-yourself projects, hobbies, off-campus lecturing, political activity, his own family, and so on. Or, paradoxically, he may be so engrossed in administrative activities on the campus, so absorbed in the work of faculty committees, so occupied with matters of public relations, so busy being what the students like to call a "wheel," that he has little time or energy left over for the mere human beings who compose his classes.

Negligence or indifference (from whatever cause) in teaching is widespread, well recognized, and generally tolerated or even encouraged in the universities. Only in the most flagrant cases of absenteeism or neglect does anybody (from the president and the dean on down) venture to suggest that the professor ought to pay more attention to his teaching duties. Indeed, the professor who pays too much attention to his teaching duties is definitely suspect on the campuses of most major universities. People wonder whether he is a good researcher who may get the university's name in the learned journals, or an aggressive personality who may win good publicity for the university in the public prints. Of course, something may be said for the negligent or indifferent professor. Often he cares so little about teaching that he does not bother to give "a good stiff course" in which he distributes many bad grades; instead he allows his classes to run themselves, more or less, and leaves the students to their own devices, some to learn and some to fritter away time. On the other hand, these negligent and indifferent professors are often just the ones who insist most emphatically (for rather obvious psychological reasons) that their students "get down to business."

A final reason for poor teaching among the professors is lack of a personality that can put itself in rapport with many types of student personality, understand how to interest and stimulate young minds, and perceive the many facets that many minds may discover in most types of human knowledge. Too many professors are cynics who can do nothing but ridicule the ignorance of students; too many are determined factualists who beat down imagination and creativeness; too many are "disciplinarians" who think that classrooms and the process of learning should never be any fun to students; too many are academicians whose thinking moves always in formal grooves and who are quite unable to comprehend differences of interpretation; too many have such high regard for "truth" that they discourage all independent thought for fear that the young person may be "wrong"; too many, insensitive to the feelings of other people, or unsympathetic toward universal human weaknesses, antagonize students permanently by unjustly accusing them of cheating, refusing to believe or to accept honest excuses for absences or late work, making no allowances for normal human lapses of attention or deviations from the straight-and-narrow path of industry; too many of them have developed (as a re-

sult of early maladjustments and insecurities) an inferiority complex that results in certain typical personality
traits, including compensatory arrogance, morbid suspicion, fear that students will discover professorial weaknesses, timidity that masks itself as unfriendliness, intolerance of disagreement, sometimes downright sadism.
To be sure, professors are not the only people in our
society likely to have the personality weaknesses mentioned here. But professors are likely (for reasons outlined
in a previous chapter) to have more of them than other
people; and besides, they are so situated that their personality weaknesses, by operating on students at a very
impressionable period of life, can do immeasurably more
harm than those of most other people.

Upholding the Standards

Since the Russians scared the wits out of us with their
sputniks, we have been hearing a continuous uproar in
the public press, in educational circles, and in legislative
halls, about the need for raising the standards of American
education. I have already said that a very large number
of professors are honestly convinced that the only way to
"uphold the standards of the university" is to give many
bad grades.

There is a story that Professor E. G. Lorenzen, of Yale
University's law school, while acting as a visiting professor at another college, inquired about this college's
grading policies. The Dean answered, "Flunk as many as
you want." To which Professor Lorenzen replied, "I don't
flunk my students. I teach them."

But I myself, in thirty-five years as a faculty member
of universities, have yet to hear one faculty member say
in open faculty meeting that the best way to "uphold the

standards of the university" is to be a skillful and inspiring teacher. Instead, there is continual talk about "tightening the curriculum," "more efficient procedures for the selection of applicants for admission," "increasing the course load," "greater concentration on major subjects," and similar matters, together with complaints about the "inefficiency of the high schools," the "hopelessness of competing with TV," or even "the incurable stupidity of the human race." I have never heard any professor suggest that the failure of a student is also the failure of his professor. The two or three professors I still remember from my own student days as outstanding persons, scholars, and teachers, almost never found it necessary to give a failing grade to any student. And now that I myself am a professor, I never set down a failing grade for a student without a feeling of contrition and humiliation. I feel that, through ignorance or lack of skill or indifference or selfishness, I have betrayed some young person who was depending on me. I am ashamed that I have not "upheld the standards of the university."

If a teacher is a good teacher he ought to be able to make his students understand what he is trying to tell them. The students are all about the same age, have similar educational backgrounds, and (if they have graduated honestly from high school) are essentially intelligent. If he fails to make them understand, so that a considerable portion of them fail, or almost fail, he is almost certainly a poor teacher. But try to get anybody around a university to admit to such a heresy! In all my years of teaching, I have known of only one professor whose savage failing-rate (over 50 per cent of his class) was questioned by the authorities of the university; but even they did not question him because they lacked faith in his teaching ability, but because he was bringing some very unfavorable publicity to his department.

It is true that a professor may be an excellent teacher and able to make his students understand the course, yet assign them such a heavy load of work that only a few of them can complete it. For example, he may teach them how to solve a certain type of long problem, but then assign them fifty such problems to complete overnight; or he may give them an excellent understanding of a historical period, but then assign them 5000 pages of source material to be read in one week. By making such assignments, and giving poor or failing grades to the students who do not complete them, he fancies that he is "upholding the standards of the university." But here we encounter once more that schizophrenic trait that is so common among professors. Presumably the university exists for the purpose of educating students; but if the "standards" of the university (in this case, the load of work required) eliminate a large number of students from the university, the whole purpose of the university is defeated. Yet universities seem proud of this inconsistency.

The professorial mind seldom seems to realize (or perhaps it just doesn't care) that dropping a student on account of failure may solve a troublesome problem for the professor here and now. But a student who has failed, and is dropped from the course or from the university, is *not* a solved problem. In relation to his own future career, and in relation to society at large (which is supplying the the money for the university) the student who has failed is a more serious problem than ever. A student who can do only 25 problems out of the assigned 50, or who can read only 2500 pages out of the assigned 5000, is by no means a total loss to himself or to society; yet (having completed only 50 per cent of his assigned work) he is dropped from the rolls. His life, and his possible future contribution to society, have been considered less important than the necessity of "upholding the standards of the university." He has become a sacrifice to a vague and abstract "high standard" arbitrarily set by his professors. I do not perceive how such a sacrifice can be justified either from a democratic, humane, individualistic point of view, or from a nationalistic, socialistic, utilitarian point of view. In these days of increasingly intense competition with the Communist world, our nation cannot afford to let even a little of its brain-power go to waste.

If all of us who are in any way concerned with higher education would remember that "high standards" which large numbers of students cannot live up to mean only one of two things — either that the professor involved is a poor teacher, or that he is making unrealistically heavy assignments — we might be a little more successful than we have been in improving the quality of higher education in America. Practically everybody seems to think that a university has demonstrated its "high standards" when a large number of its students make poor grades, or fail completely. It is an almost hopeless task to try to make anybody (especially the professors) see that a university in which large numbers of students make poor grades, or fail, actually has very low standards of teaching, or a very unrealistic (and even dangerous) comprehension of its function as an educational institution in a democracy — a democracy threatened, as never before in its history, by the growing power of a hostile nation.

Immorality among the Professors

What the universities, and the professors themselves,

can do about all these weaknesses will be suggested in a later chapter of this book. The nub of the whole matter, however, for both the university administration and the professor, is to have the desire for better teaching, or at any rate to establish better teaching as an ideal more significant than it now is in the university world. Much could be accomplished by a mere arbitrary, deliberate, officially announced and publicly supported change in administrative policy.

The majority of professors are not actually bad men; they do not *want* to do evil. But the whole university community fails, as a rule, to see that the obligation of good teaching is essentially a moral obligation. When any man sees another human being in need of help, and can help him, and does not help him, but passes by on the other side, that man is immoral. This is even more acutely true if the passer-by is an adult, and the human being in need of help is a young person. Even elephants, wild cattle, and baboons band together to protect their collective young. It does seem as if college professors (and university administrations) could demonstrate as much morality as elephants, cattle, and baboons. But a very large percentage of college professors (and university administrations) do not practice that much morality. A very large percentage of them make no special effort to help their fellow man in ways that are almost more important than matters of life and death, for though to save a man's life is important, to give him a life worth saving is almost equally important. When generations of young people come to university professors asking to be shown how to have a life worth saving, and are turned away because the professors are willing accessories to the formalism of examinations-grades-credits systems, or

because the professors think that "upholding the standards of the university" by giving bad grades is more
virtuous than good teaching, or insist that learning be unpleasant, or are selfishly busy or negligent or indifferent,
or are dominated by certain character traits that are
harmful to young people but that can be altered, these
professors are being immoral. The only way they could
be more immoral would be to commit murder.

This immorality of the professors and of the universities is widespread, and it is growing. The universities
are leading no moral revivals these days. Instead, the
moral revivals are being led by ecclesiastical showmen,
religious quacks, leaders of cults, well-meaning but abys-
mally ignorant missionaries, and all the other ragtag and
bobtail of sensationalism and superstition. This is not as
it should be. The professors and the universities should
be showing the way to a higher and more universal
morality. But they lack the will and the spirit for it. They
should have got the habit of morality in their own classrooms; but it is there that the majority of them daily
commit almost the worst of immoralities. This is a basic
tragedy of modern America.

CHAPTER SIX

MANY INVENTIONS

Acutely aware of the failure of a large percentage of their students, the universities have "sought out many inventions" to try to reduce the number of these failures. Most of these inventions are old familiar devices that the universities have been playing with, like an old pack of cards, for years. They involve changes in course requirements for certain majors or certain degrees, changes in textbooks, changes in laboratory requirements, changes in credit distribution, and so on. These efforts at improvement amount to little more than shuffling the old cards and dealing out new hands. Invariably they are directed toward the student, not the professor or at the professor's system of teaching or at the university's own ideals as to what constitutes a good professor and good teaching. But, just to be fair, I should like to devote this chapter to an examination of some of the newer inventions the universities have tried.

But first, a word in behalf of the student. Even under the protective cover of shallow cynicism and bored sophistication, or even when he is just a nice and conventional high school graduate, the typical freshman is an enthusiastic, hopeful, and eagerly idealistic youth. He has a vague inkling of what the university *ought* to do for him, and a tremendous faith. He thinks he will find here what he has been subconsciously looking for and preparing for all his short life: the solution to the mysteries in which he has been lost, the opportunity to find himself and to realize himself completely.

Perhaps away from home for the first time, always in a brand-new world, dreaming of accomplishing miracles, determined to make a "success" of his life, he is ready for the highest adventure. One of my students put it like this:

A young mind. A brilliant young mind.
An eager mind, coiled to spring upon some bit of
    knowledge

And devour it,
And so grow.

A probing mind, wanting to know the answer,
Or how to ask the question.
An intelligent mind, fitting together bits of knowl-
    edge
Into coherent form.

A strong mind, not unwilling to do
The Disagreeable,
The Tedious,
The Dangerous.

An open mind, ready to be
Convinced,
Disillusioned,
Distressed. . . .

In consideration of the various factors involved

In re curricular adjustments might I state that
The overall program must be converted from the
Perspective of schoolparentteacher relationship,
Never forgetting that each of the parts which con-
stitute
The general scheme employed must be approached
At all times to cultivate a satisfactory
Environment. . . .

What are we going to have to know for the test?
Well, run over your Place-names and Dates and People to Remember.
What's the test going to be like?
Truefalse thirty per cent multiplechoice thirty percent matching thirty percent essay questions ten
percent.
What percent of our final grade will this test count?
Each six weeks' test counts twenty percent of your
semester grade. The semester final counts forty
percent, but if you have say a D going into the
final and you get a high A on the final and your
participation has been good you'll be able to pull
the D up to a B.
Will you let us do make-up work if we get an F?
Yes, but that will only bring an F up to a D
and it goes back down to an F if you don't get a C
on the fifth six-weeks' test or on the final.
Now, let's see. . . .

This is a quick sketch of what happens to the enthusiasm and the idealism of the freshman. Do the universities crush the enthusiasm and the idealism out of
malice aforethought?

Well, sometimes yes; but more often no. The universities are like a man who has left moth balls in his pockets, and wonders why other people avoid him. The universities see that the students are not learning successfully, and they are seeking out many inventions that may help the situation. But, like the man with the moth balls, they try everything except removal of the real source of the offense.

Screening the Applicants

One of the newer inventions consists of more and more strenuous efforts by the university to screen applicants for admission to the freshman class, and to admit only those judged to be of the highest quality. The prospective student must run a gauntlet of watchdogs that seem to be actually trying to keep him out of the university. The authorities demand transcripts, interviews, special credits, recommendations, photographs; they administer achievement tests, intelligence tests, aptitude tests, College Entrance Board examinations, physical examinations. The prospective freshman is not allowed to say, as he once was: "Please, sir, I know I am young and ignorant. But I want to learn. I am willing to spend a great deal of time, effort, and money in order to learn. Will you teach me?" It should be as simple as that. But the very struggle required to be allowed even to enter a university nowadays is so stupendous that it would discourage anybody but hopeful and ambitious youth. And the effort required is becoming greater and greater every year, the hurdles higher, the barriers more complicated, the red tape more endless and sticky. All of it was originally intended to make our universities more effective. Not only has it clearly failed in this aim, but also it leaves with the prospective student and with society at large the smoldering suspicion that the universities are quietly organizing themselves as an intellectual Fifth Column refusing to aid the common people. It is not surprising that, in turn, the common people often seem anti-intellectual.

But insofar as the individual student is concerned, the truly sad element in all this maze of ritual required for admission to the university is the fact that the student is impressed, from the very beginning, with a false set of values. He sees that the university-entrance people value, above everything else, tests, grades, credits. They care nothing for originality, imagination, creativeness; they do not ask whether the student will use selfishly or unselfishly the learning he may acquire at the university; or whether he has a mind capable not merely of absorbing learning, but of synthesizing it so that he may emerge from the university with a mind and a personality altogether better than those he brought with him; or whether he has a fundamentally adaptable or an unadaptable mind, an independent or a conventional mind, a courageous or a timid nature, imaginative or only imitative capacity. It is precisely these things that really matter — and it is precisely these things that the university entrance people ignore.

How can the impressionable young person fail to be impressed? How can he fail to believe, along with these grand university people, that the only things that really matter in the world are tests, grades, credits? Unless something like a miracle happens (as it does indeed happen to 10 to 15 per cent of the college students) he is lost forever, an idolater worshiping tests, grades, credits, even before he attends his first class.

The members of the admissions committee, knowing in their hearts how badly their universities are failing to educate most of the students, and doggedly persisting in the belief that the fault lies in the "material" they get from the high schools rather than in the universities themselves, labor conscientiously to acquire the "best" possible material for the freshman classes. But having found that, despite all their labors, the universities are still failing, they have come in desperation, after all the high school grades have been reviewed, the tests taken, and the results graded, to depend on evidence of a student's "outside activities" in high school to help them make their decisions. A student who has made high grades, and who has also been an athlete, a band member, a debater, a cheerleader, an actor, an officer in some student organization, is always chosen in preference to a student with an equally high scholastic record, but no record of "outside activities." The admissions committee wants "well-rounded" students.

This is most curious. Just why, of all possible qualifications for admission, this one should have been chosen out of a hat, as it were, is a mystery. Naturally, a good argument could be put up for the "well-rounded" student. But an equally good argument could be put up for the highly specialized student. As a matter of fact, it is proverbial that the jack-of-all-trades is good at none, that the cobbler should stick to his last, that the secret of success is singleness of purpose. This is not intended to belittle the "well-rounded" student; much can be said for him. Yet the chances are ten to one that the members of the admissions committee themselves were not "well-rounded" youths in high school. Probably they were studious, bookish, not politically popular on the campus, not active participants in class functions, athletics, and all the other side-show activities of high school. The chances are, furthermore, that the university's own alumni

who are famous in the world of science and of scholarship were not "well-rounded" students when they were
at the university, but, far more probably, were people
who had little time for extracurricular activities, and little
real delight in anything but their studies. Furthermore
(though I do not know whether this is statistically veri-
fiable), my own observations indicate that most people
do not become truly and admirably "well rounded" until
after they have perfected themselves in some specialized
field.

Then, after these "well-rounded" students are accepted into the university, what happens? The professors
begin telling them to "pay attention to business," and "not
to be distracted by the unessentials," and "to learn to con-
centrate." They are admonished, in the widely quoted
words of Professor Howard Mumford Jones, that "Learning is a lonely process, fundamentally asocial despite all
our easy talk about well-adjusted personalities." It is all
most incredibly paradoxical, and a symptom of that schizophrenia, mentioned so often in this book, that bedevils
all higher education in America.

Greetings to the Freshman

As soon as the student has weathered the admissions
committee, and has been accepted as a freshman, he finds
himself involved still more deeply in a maze of credit
systems and official requirements that the university has
slowly built up, over the years, in a determined effort to
make its work seem less futile, its educative process less
a failure.

The freshman, having first been told in the Dean's
welcoming address that he is now a university member
who must act with responsibility; having been told in

the President's solemn matriculation address that he is no longer a child, but an adult who is expected to act with independence and self-reliance; having been told by officers and representatives of various student organizations that he has now become a member of a self-governing community in all of whose rights and privileges he may participate; having been told all this — that he must be responsible, independent, self-reliant, self-governing — the inspired freshman turns by chance to the university catalogue, and reads (I quote verbatim from the first catalogue I pick up):

REQUIREMENTS FOR

THE DEGREE OF

BACHELOR OF ARTS

English 601 or 601Q, and six semester hours of sophomore . . . six semester hours of mathematics . . . a student may substitute . . . some majors do not permit this substitution. See requirements under "C" below . . . twelve semester hours in the natural sciences, including six semester hours . . . special departmental requirements will be found under "D, 8" below . . . six semester hours in Government . . . six semester hours in History 615 or six advanced semester hours . . . the requirements set down below under "Majors and Minors" . . . thirty-six semester hours of advanced courses.

See "Course Numbers" in *General Information Bulletin.* Not more than twelve of the thirty-six hours of advanced courses may be taken . . . eighteen of these thirty-six hours must be . . . at least eighteen hours of advanced courses, including six . . . at least twelve semester hours of elective work must be taken

in subjects outside the major and minor fields . . .
not more than thirty-six hours may be counted . . .
majors require twenty-four semester hours . . .
minors as listed under the major subject . . . first
minor twelve semester hours . . . second minor six
semester hours in a field supporting the first minor
or the major . . . a student must make (a) an average
of at least fifteen points per semester . . . and (b) at
least fifteen points per semester hour . . . an A grade
counts as 21 points, a *B* as 18 points, a *C* as 15 points
. . . the student must, not later than three weeks
before the end of the term or semester . . . the
student is strongly advised . . . the student will note
that it is necessary . . .

This is what faces the student who has just been informed thrice over by the highest authorities that he is
now a responsible, independent, self-reliant, self-governing adult.

Obviously, the emphasis here is quite ridiculously
wrong; and, as Henry Adams has said, "The chief wonder
of education is that it does not ruin everybody concerned
with it, teacher and taught." As a matter of fact, it does
ruin many of them completely, and nearly all of them in
some ways.

Even though it be argued (quite falsely, of course) that
this system of credits achieved through examinations and
grades (all of it so complexly organized that only an ac-
countant, a lawyer, or a university registrar could possibly
comprehend it) has the eventual result of somehow magi-
cally producing the "right" kind of student, the student
does not know this. All that he knows is that the faculty
and the administration demand certain specific examina-

tions, grades, and credits. The faculty and the administration must know what is best in higher education; therefore, the student too thinks that examinations, grades, and credits are the most important thing in the world.

In every university I know anything about, and among all university students I know, the dominating element in the student's relation to his education is — the grade. The grade so overshadows everything else that the student will suffer, scheme, lie, and cheat for it. And when he has it, he is content. The professor who tries, however modestly, to break with the grade-and-credit system is incomprehensible to the student, and meets only blank stares when he suggests that the grade-and-credit system emphasizes the unessential and the spurious in education. What else, the student wants to know, is worth working for except grades and credits? If he chances to "gun" an examination, and make a higher grade than he knows his real knowledge warrants, he is jubilant; his lack of knowledge does not trouble him. Or if he chances to make a bad grade, he may be heartbroken, not because his knowledge was small, but because the grade was. He can never understand, any more than can the typical professor, that the grade-and-credit system is a distortion and substitution of basic values.

What About Small Classes?

Another invention meant to improve the universities has aimed at increasing the faculty-student ratio. Insofar as this represents an effort to treat the student as an individual instead of an element in a system, it is commendable. But too often this reform stops short of the real solution of the problem. If a professor is a poor teacher, or a personality warped in ways that have already been discussed in this book, it is an excellent thing to have the fewest possible students exposed to him. On the other hand, if he is a good teacher, it is unfortunate that he touches the lives of so few students. Thus, unless the university strives to procure good teachers, its expensive policy of bestowing benefits with one hand ends in its removing the benefits with the other hand.

In my own undergraduate days, the two or three best teachers I had (the ones whom I most wanted to be like, who inspired me to want to know more about their subjects, and who altered my fundamental thought-patterns most profoundly) presided over very large classes; and (by accident, I am sure) the very worst teacher I ever had presided over a class of four students, of whom I was one. Today I know professors who seldom spend time in personal conferences but who are an inspiration to all their students; and I know other professors who confer personally with their students far above and beyond the call of duty, but are so dogmatic, authoritarian, impolite, or pedantic in conferences that their students hate them and their courses. Students often confuse the personality of the professor with the subject he is teaching, and are attracted to or repelled from learning in direct ratio to their liking and respect for the professor. Accordingly, the theory that the student progresses in direct ratio to the amount of time his professor can give to him individually is not always, or even often, correct. It all depends on the professor.

Reviewing more than fifty years of research in this field, the *Encyclopedia of Educational Research* (1950) concludes (in typical educationist jargon, to be sure): "On the basis of criteria used in the experimental studies published to date and under typical groups of teaching procedures, mere size of class has little significant influence on educational efficiency as measured by achievement in the academic subjects." The real beneficiary of small classes is the professor. On the other hand, if the professor (relieved of the burden of large classes) has time to devote to his own research, he may discover and accomplish things in scholarship and science that make students respect him more, and therefore do better work under him; and he may bring such credit to his university that the student feels stimulated by merely being a part of a learned community having a superior reputation. These benefits of small classes, however, operate only indirectly on the student, and depend on the quality of the professor.

What Shall Be Taught?

President Hutchins' experiment with the University of Chicago was another of the many inventions designed to make the American university less of a failure. Though, as a whole, the experiment did not meet the approval of American educators, it did have an influence in making professors everywhere think, for a change, about education. Moreover, Chicago's emphasis on the more liberal, classical, and basic aspects of learning, instead of mere technical skill or practical knowledge, has influenced the curricula of most American universities. The pragmatic drift toward vocationalism and early professionalism was halted; and most educators came to believe that, in the words of the President's Commission on Higher Education (1947), "The first goal in education for democracy is the full, rounded, and continuing development of the person. . . . To liberate and perfect the intrinsic powers of every citizen is the central purpose of democracy, and its furtherance of individual self-realization is its greatest glory."

Nevertheless, the Chicago practices, even in modified form, do not seem to have accomplished the results hoped for. The universities are still, by their own records, succeeding completely with only a small portion of their students.

It seems that what is needed is not so much a change in the curriculum as a change in the methods of presenting the curriculum. A good scholar and a good teacher could make a far more meaningful, instructive, and inspiring course out of teaching the history of the ABC's than a good scholar and a poor teacher could make out of the whole of Greek philosophy. *What* is taught matters far less than *who* teaches it.

Joining the Disjointed

In an uncommon mood of self-analysis and self-criticism, the universities have noted a certain divisive, disjunctive tendency among their students. The students do not form an intellectually sympathetic and mutually understanding body. It is said that, in a world that grows more interdependent every day, students are developing no social sense, no feeling of social responsibility, no concept of working co-operatively toward valid social ideals, no understanding of the ideals and the contributions of different elements in the social structure. Accordingly, the universities, with characteristic desire for uniformity, have sought out certain inventions to remedy the divisiveness among the students.

This again represents a kind of schizophrenia; for the universities themselves continue contributing to the divisiveness by requiring students to split themselves off into "major" fields of study, where they become highly departmentalized as chemists, mathematicians, historians, and so on, and where they develop little comprehension of the methods and values of the other groups. Each department, furthermore, subdivides itself into still smaller groups. The chemists split into organic chemists, inorganic chemists, biochemists, chemical engineers; the student taking a course in Milton has little association with one studying Melville, and the specialist in medieval law never talks to the specialist in modern labor. The university, by its own requirements, becomes a collection of insulated pigeonholes into which students and scholars creep, and where they hear no echoes from other pigeonholes. The university is not, for most of the students, universal.

It should be noted that, contrary to the usual opinion, some people think that this splitting and subsplitting helps cultivate personal individuality out of what is, in so many ways, regimented uniformity within the university and within the modern world, and is therefore desirable. Other people think that it is likely to stunt and thwart the individual student's development in all ways but one, and thus make him not only a lopsided intellect, but also a narrow-minded and intolerant personality who has no sense of social responsibility, and is not adjusted to the realities of modern, highly socialized society. Still other people, their eyes on the practical necessities of life, think that, with the fields of knowledge extending to infinite horizons, the student is foolish to try to "take all knowledge for his province," but must be content with a very small private plot which he can cultivate intensively for the sake of a livelihood.

The universities have been in something of a dither as to which of these three points of view they should adopt. But in general, the universities have yielded (sometimes reluctantly and halfheartedly) to the continually increasing pressures of society, and have made some effort to patch up the disjointed student body, to break down the insulated walls between pigeonholes.

One of the means of accomplishing the unification has been the "common core" of courses. Science students have been forced to take "humanistic" courses designed to inculcate in them the ideals and values of society at large; and liberal arts students have been required to take courses in science in order to acquaint them with the ideals by which the other half lives.

For one reason or another, the common core has not proved particularly successful. The science students have been in such a hurry to accomplish tangible results, and have been so acutely aware that the young scientist must specialize if he is to succeed in his profession, that they have resented the time spent on the nonscience courses, and have discovered many ingenious ways to get around the regulations. In this they have been aided and abetted, more often than not, by the science professors themselves. Furthermore, the humanist professors do not take kindly to the teaching of reluctant and rebellious young scientists, and do not understand the values and the intellectual objectives of the scientists well enough to be successful teachers for them.

In the same way, the liberal arts majors grudgingly take the science courses, choose those that are the least scientific, generally scorn them and also what they regard as the narrow-minded ignorance of the science professors, and consider the science courses only another senseless burden of requirements enforced by the university for some unknown reason, and endured by the student only because he must endure it if he expects to graduate. The science professors, too, are impatient with the liberal arts students, think that teaching them is a shameful "popularizing" of science, and know so little about the point of view of the liberal arts students that they usually incur only the contempt of the latter.

All in all, therefore, these common-core requirements, aiming at unifying the students in a common respect for the democratic heritage and common ideals for the perfection of a democratic society, must be regarded as, for the most part, another failure of the universities.

Fairly recently a second effort to accomplish this unifying purpose has been made by certain universities organizing themselves into "colleges." It is hoped that these colleges will force specialists to rub elbows with different kinds of specialists, and so reduce intellectual exclusiveness and learned narrowmindedness. The system is too young in America to have produced, as yet, any remarkable results, one way or the other. Naturally, the people who have worked hard, and the universities that have spent large sums of money in order to establish the system are not going to admit readily that the system is a failure. Their testimony, therefore, may be discounted. The entire idea, however, sounds extremely good — provided one really wants students to be socialized and unified instead of individualized and diversified.

My own university went to much trouble and expense to establish a beautifully planned college system only last year. At the same time the entering freshman class was selected with extraordinary care. Some of the good results anticipated have undoubtedly been attained already. On the other hand, the students in the colleges found themselves subjected not only to the rules, regulations, restrictions, requirements, and sometimes necessary regimentation of the university at large, but also to an additional set of these within each college, and still another set covering the interrelationships among the colleges. It is a lucky student who can get through a year without running afoul of this network. At the same time the sideshow activities of the campus (dances, receptions, intercollege games of many sorts, and so on) have been increased manyfold.

Nevertheless, the experiment looked so promising that everyone waited eagerly to see the effect it would have on the students' grades. And everyone on the campus was shocked to find that, when the first term-end grades under the new system were tabulated, about 50 per cent *more* students went "on probation" under the new system than under the old, and about 30 per cent *fewer* students qualified for the Dean's List. It would certainly be unfair to say, at this stage, that the college system was responsible for the debacle. But it does seem obvious that the college system, directed as it is at the students, is not likely to cure a disease that lies within the professors and the university itself.

Concessions to Delight

Within the classrooms the universities have not changed in the almost forty years that I have been acquainted with them; nor has the general attitude of professor toward student changed. There is still the official insistence on hard work, attending to business, performing a duty, self-discipline, avoidance of frivolities. But, with typical schizophrenia, the universities have made the student's life outside the classroom, and away from his professors, more and more in keeping with the modern world's search for delight. A look at some of the college buildings erected since the Second World War reveals tasteful architecture, luxurious interiors of student unions, plush dormitories, attractive ways of serving food, sumptuously furnished clubrooms, and much besides that is consistent with the age in which we live. Outside the classroom the Spartan ideal has been abandoned.

Apparently the universities are willing to make concessions to the modern spirit everywhere except in the place where it really matters. Perhaps they think that extracurricular luxuries will make the students more willing to endure curricular austerities. And perhaps they are right, to a certain extent. But when one observes the really scandalous extent to which the universities are failing with their students, one is compelled to believe that the extracurricular luxuries are inadequate, after all. The core of the university is the professor in his classroom. That is where improvement is required, and that is where (despite the many inventions listed in this chapter) no improvement has occurred for at least forty years.

CHAPTER SEVEN

HOW TO GET INTO COLLEGE

IBM versus Student

Since the Second World War, practically all of the "better" universities in America have grown enthusiastic on the subject of testing high school graduates to determine who should be admitted to the universities. They give numerous kinds of tests — achievement, aptitude, intelligence, personality, and so on — with a so-called "battery" of tests (including elements of all the others) being most commonly used.

The College Entrance Board tests, and the tests issued by the mushrooming Educational Testing Service, harbored at Princeton, have become the two most popular instruments. A description of the latter service, written by William Harlan Hale, appears in the *Reporter* for October 6, 1955. Even though this description includes certain elements of caricature, it contains, like all good caricature, essential truth. The Educational Testing Service, like others that have sprung up in response to the current demand, is a vast mechanized organization whose soul is an array of IBM machines operating on assembly line methods and with a complete and purposed elimination of the human factor at the level of the examiner, the examined, and the grader. The prospective freshman answers questions on the test by marking blank spaces with a metallic pencil; the IBM machine gobbles up all papers, whirls them through magnetic counters, and produces a score that reveals the student's intellect, interest, aptitudes, and character, and by inference predicts his fate in the university — all with that infallible accuracy possible only for electronic devices.

I confess to taking a bleak view of all testing devices that imply prediction of the student's success in the university. This skepticism is based on long personal observation and on experiments. I have noticed, for example, that the testers nearly always come up with negative, indefinite, debatable, contradictory, or vaguely positive results, and then explain that, if conditions had not been just so-and-so, or if such-and-such an element had been considered, or if this-or-that difficulty had not intervened, or if certain improvements were made in the testing device, the results would certainly have had greater predictive value. The testers have been saying this, to my personal knowledge, for over thirty years; and they are still saying it. Life just refuses to co-operate with electronics.

Several years ago my own university gave the Educational Testing Service's battery of tests (American Council of Education Psychological Examination, General Achievement Tests, and tests on expression and reading comprehension) to 400-odd randomly selected freshmen at the beginning of two successive years. Subsequent investigation into the university history of these subjects revealed *absolutely no reliable correlation* between the grades made on the tests and the grades made in the university.

Furthermore, all the major systems of testing admittedly deal with *probabilities* involving *groups* — not with *facts* involving *individuals;* that is, even if they should be reliable for considerable majorities within certain large groups, they cannot be trusted for any specified individual. Yet it is always specified individual human beings that university admissions committees are (or ought to be) interested in. The testers, the admissions commitees, do not seem to realize this fact. That is why the results of the tests and the actual results in the university correlate so badly. To illustrate this lack of correlation, let me quote from a typical report, one of any number that might be cited. This one is from a study of graduates at Hunter College:

> When the records of the students in the highest and lowest quartiles of the class [at Hunter], as determined by scholastic index at college graduation, are compared in respect to admissions records, it is obvious that high scores at entrance do not guarantee college success in individual cases, nor do low scores doom a student to academic obscurity.
>
> Three students whose class averages on admission were as high as 92 or 93, an additional student whose Regents [examination by the University of the State of New York] was 94, and one who scored at the 99th percentile on the American Council of Education Tests were to be found in the lowest quarter of the class upon graduation. Conversely, a student who had a [high school] class average on admission of 73 was graduated *cum laude,* and one who had a Regents average of 77 and who was placed in the lowest twentieth of the class on the American Council of

Education tests was in the highest quarter of the class on graduation . . . .

The same story can be told in another way. Seventy-eight students at graduation were awarded high scholastic honors. These included election to Phi Beta Kappa and the awarding of graduation and department honors. Among these seventy-eight can be found some who on admission presented close to the minimum acceptable class averages and some who on the American Council of Education tests showed in the lowest quartile.

Furthermore, very large numbers of those who entered college with the highest averages graduated from college in the second and third quartiles of their class, and many of those who entered with the lowest averages graduated in the same second and third quartiles. Finally, different criteria for judging high school graduates did not correlate among themselves in predicting college success; and correlations computed according to major fields of specialization were still more contradictory.

The fact is that a very great majority of high school students, though not specially gifted, will do reasonably well (if given opportunity and motivation) in choosing work for which they have average aptitude, and will succeed reasonably well at that work. The nation is filled with successful doctors, lawyers, teachers, engineers, bankers, and businessmen whom the testing systems would not have rated among the highest on graduation from high school, and would not originally have approved for the work they are in. Thus, a highly successful banker of my acquaintance entered the university with average good grades; made one F, a D, and three C's on his first report card in the university; graduated with four A's and one

B and was so outstanding in philosophy that he was offered a fellowship in that subject when he graduated. Many a person engages in some work only because of parental pressure, accident, expediency, or the desire for money, and yet manages to muddle through it with credit and satisfaction to himself and profit to the community. Likewise, many a person not specially gifted comes to college with only average test grades to recommend him, finds his interest aroused somehow, and becomes a superior student, or else loses what interest he had, and becomes a poor or mediocre student. Prediction in any individual case is impossible; and it is reliable in large groups with only the lowest 10 to 20 per cent. In other words, the entrance tests may be trusted to eliminate the completely hopeless (along with a few who would do well in college if given the chance); but their efficacy as predictive instruments seems to extend no further.

Recently 1400 prep and high school graduates applied for admission to Amherst College; and the admissions authorities declared that at least 1200 (85 per cent) of them were "clearly qualified" for admission. Every admissions committee at every college and university in the country is faced with just such a situation. That is to say, a very large percentage of all persons who have finished high school honestly are "clearly qualified" to succeed in some form of higher education.

This is why testing agencies can boast of the success of their work, and why universities are likely to feel that their methods of selecting students are satisfactory. They can hardly go wrong when 85 per cent of the applicants are "clearly qualified" in any event. On the other hand, if the testing systems indicate probable failure, and the university rejects the student in question, nobody can ever prove that the systems were wrong. Finally, if the testing systems make a favorable report, and the university accepts the student, and he fails out of the university, it is just one of those things; nobody can expect to be right in every single case; and there are always extenuating circumstances or peculiar facts that explain the failure.

Time after time I have known students who would not have been admitted to certain universities on their high school records and test grades, but who were admitted because their fathers were notable benefactors of the university, or were on the university faculty. Yet these students do just as well as the average student who is admitted on the basis of records and test grades. There was one case in which I pulled all the wires I could, exerted all the influence I could, to get a young man admitted to my university, even though he would not have had the ghost of a chance if someone had not been speaking for him. He was finally admitted. When he eventually graduated, he was the top student in his division, and was granted a $1500 scholarship for foreign study.

What the testing systems do is to discover the 15 to 20 per cent of high school graduates who are not bona fide graduates — those who have been given a diploma only because they were good athletes, or because a father was head of the local school board, or because they were sweet and obedient children who never gave anybody any trouble, or because the high school teachers merely grew tired of seeing them around. But as for all the others, I cannot see that testing has any predictive significance in any individual case, and only a very slight predictive significance (if any at all) in large groups and averages. The universities spend a great deal of time and money selecting their freshmen . . . yet, sadly and strangely, university students continue to fail, go on probation, and drop out at the customary rate, and only 10 to 15 per cent of them continue to be wholly satisfactory.

Why Tests Fail

The chief weakness of the testing systems is that they cannot measure either a student's motivation or his ability to withstand the ordinary pressures, shocks, and temptations of life. I have known students who made superior records for a year, or two, or three, and then failed miserably because they were having an unhappy love affair, or their parents were getting a divorce, or their best friend withdrew to attend another university, or they felt resentful toward their major professor for some real or fancied injustice, or they spent too much time on their favorite course, or they succumbed to the influence of drink, gambling, or immoral women. The systems are unable to deal with these all-important realities of life. They do not even profess to do so. Their sole purpose is to indicate *potentialities*. But, as every parent and every teacher knows, incredibly high potentialities exist in practically *all* young people. "If we all lived up to the promises of our infancy," said Schiller, "we should all be geniuses." The trick is not to find young people with potentialities (that is easy), but to get them to realize their potentialities. Every parent and every teacher knows that the young people with the highest potentialities are not the greatest successes in college or in life. Students with only mediocre potentialities who are properly motivated and who are relatively immune to ordinary pressures and temptations, are the ones who most often succeed. Very rarely (as Professor Catherine M. Cox, of Stanford, has shown) do true geniuses have remarkably high I.Q.'s. And the student "most likely to succeed" seldom makes a resounding success.

Another weakness of the testing systems is that they cannot measure those qualities which, after all, are the ones that secure success in the university and in life. Even the will and the ability to make good grades in impersonal subjects like physics and mathematics depends on the student's will and ability to make adjustments to university life, to his classmates, and to his professors. And these adjustments depend, in turn, on qualities that do not appear in the blank spaces filled in with a metallic pencil and run through an IBM machine — qualities like dress, tact, courtesy, humor, consideration for others, physical appearance, voice, accent, personal habits, willingness to compromise, self-confidence, health, and a dozen others. A dirty, rude, coarse youth with a greasy complexion, a whiny voice, a rural accent, a known determination to have his rights down to the last half a point on every quiz, and a habit of spraying in the face of the person to whom he talks has two strikes against him even before the professor grades his paper. This kind of student will never be a success in the university (no matter what intellectual potentialities he may have) so long as his professors and his classmates can prevent it.

The test has not yet been devised that can measure all these matters; therefore the test has not yet been devised that can predict any student's success in college.

In the face of all this that seems so obvious, it is extraordinary that university admissions committees still seem satisfied with their work. If their university is a small institution with a restricted student body, they are certain that some of the people they rejected are "clearly qualified" to enter, and are perhaps just as good material as that accepted, or even better. There is simply no way of comparing human beings as you would compare pins. A *B* student coming from a family background where learning is valued may be a better prospect than an *A* student coming from a family that does not have a book in the house, and doesn't really care whether or not he does well in his studies. And who can tell whether the top-ranking graduate from a high school graduating thirty students is better or worse than the top-ranking student from a high school graduating three hundred? There are a thousand such combinations and permutations, and the admissions committee of a small, exclusive school cannot know which of all possible combinations and permutations should weigh most heavily. Nevertheless, and in spite of the fact that one third, at least, of the people they accept into the university will never graduate, and that another third will have serious scholastic difficulties before finally graduating, the admissions committees will continue to maintain that they are doing a good job.

In large state institutions where there are few restrictions on the number of freshmen to be admitted, the committee is even better satisfied with the system. It will argue that no potentially good material has been discarded, and that all of it has been discovered. There is no way of actually proving that these assumptions are wrong, for if the student never gets a chance to attend the university, nobody can tell whether he would have succeeded there. The admissions committee is much more likely to say that any error it has made lies in admitting students who were not really qualified for university work, as evidenced by the long term-end lists of students on probation, students withdrawn from the university, and students dropped because of scholastic failures. Therefore the committee goes back with renewed vigor to its testing, tries new "batteries," draws lines tighter — and inevitably ends with the same long lists of students on probation, students withdrawn, and students dropped. What else could it expect? If something like 85 per cent of the applicants are "clearly qualified" in any event, any mere random selection from among them would have as much chance of being right as would the most careful examining. All this is speculation, of course; there are no statistics. The only sure thing is that the number of failures and part-failures in the universities does not diminish with the continual "perfection" of the systems of testing for admission.

One other point should be suggested here. If many accepted applicants do not live up to *good* expectations, it is quite possible that many rejected applicants might not have lived up to *bad* expectations if they had been admitted.

Only Time Tells

The high school records and the testing systems do not and cannot take account of a student's maturing in a completely unpredictable way. Indeed, if it is true (and it seems biologically true at any rate) that the most intelligent animals are the longest in maturing, it may be possible that the students who are not the brightest at 18 may be the brightest of all at 25. I think every college professor must have noted how a student who is only fair, or even poor, as a freshman may turn out to be a top-ranking student as a senior; or how a fair or poor student who drops out of college for a year or two returns to become a top-ranking student.

Just now a young man was in my office who, three years

ago, was admitted to my university on an athletic scholarship. He never would have been admitted had he not been an athlete. He was a freshman in one of my classes that term, and I have seldom seen anyone whom I considered more hopelessly stupid. He told me today that, two weeks before he entered the university as a freshman, his mother had died. With the pride of youth, the freshman had not told me of his loss. The following summer he was hurt in an automobile accident, and had to remain out of school a year. He returned this year, and is now one of the top students in my sophomore class of 150 students.

Tomorrow night my wife and I are having dinner with a young married woman and her husband. Five years ago she failed out of the university with four F's and a D. After three years' absence she returned, and last year made three A's and two B's.

Five years ago a young woman in my freshman class seemed to me a thoroughly average student. That year she made four C's and a B-minus. She married at the end of her sophomore year, stayed out two years, and returned to finish her college education. As a senior, she made two A-pluses and three A's.

Twenty years ago I dissuaded a young man from taking one of my courses; his previous record in a similar course was much too unimpressive. Today he is a figure of almost international importance in that same field — and I cannot take the slightest credit for his success!

Twenty-five years ago I became acquainted with a young man because, in his freshman year, he was having such serious difficulties with his courses that he required the special attention of the university authorities. At last he graduated with slightly better than mediocre grades.

Today he is head of a scientific laboratory engaged in research for the Federal government, and has made contributions to science that have fundamentally changed the direction of most study in his field.

I could go on and on cataloguing such cases. Nor are they the exception that prove the rule. They *are* the rule. It is simply impossible for any testing device to predict with certainty whether a bright youth of 18 is going to mature into a brighter and brighter individual, or remain merely a bright youth of 18 all his life.

Predicting the Future from the Past

The oldest type of test for applicants to college is the *scholastic achievement test* — which purports to measure the student's proficiency in particular subjects he has studied (like algebra, history, English, and so on). Though the results of this kind of test are sometimes misleading (because the student was sick or frightened or otherwise nervously upset on the day of the test; or because, as sometimes happens, some of the questions chance to deal with one little portion of the course which the student just happens to know, or not to know, very well; or because the person who made out the test did not know how to phrase his questions clearly or choose representative or comprehensive questions), the scholastic achievement test is fairly efficient in accomplishing what it professes to accomplish; that is, the measuring of past achievement in certain subjects.

On the other hand, predicting a student's *future* success in the university from the success of his *past* achievements is not yet possible. This is one reason why the modern university is almost everywhere de-emphasizing the achievement test as a criterion for admission to the university. Many a student who did well in high school may prove a failure in college. For example, it often happens that a student who did excellent work in high school algebra and geometry bogs down in trigonometry or calculus; or a student who was a star pupil in English grammar and sentence construction may be utterly incapable of writing an original and well-constructed paper in freshman English in the university.

The scholastic achievement test may show two things. One is that the student is properly "prepared" to comprehend what he is taught in the university. Actually, however, it is of no great significance (as I have said previously) that a student is well "prepared" for the university unless he plans to enter some field which requires a sound mathematical foundation. The only preparation the student needs for most of his courses in the university is the ability to read clear English and write fairly "correct" English. This is the reason, by the way, that it has been discovered again and again that the least inaccurate single test purporting to predict success in the university is the test involving the acquaintanceship with the meanings and the uses of words.

It should be mentioned, however, that good teaching in the university may often correct deficiencies in the student's English, and the student's own maturing process may effect the same result. It is commonplace in university records to find that a student who has made poor or mediocre grades in freshman English may make excellent grades in junior or senior English courses. It is commonplace, moreover, to find that students who were poor in freshman English later on become highly successful journalists, editors, novelists, and playwrights. With good instruction, a student may continue learning for years.

The second thing that the scholastic achievement test may show is a little of the personality of the student. The person who proves that he has been able to achieve a certain amount of knowledge in high school, proves also that he has a good memory, a certain kind of patient persistence, and obedient behavior, all of which qualities will serve him well in his university career. It is the indirect evidence, attained by means of the scholastic achievement test, of the presence of these qualities in a student that has made this type of test one of the most reliable predicters of university success. (Perhaps it is no glowing tribute to the university that a student who has only good memory, patient persistence, and obedient behavior is likely to make good in the university.)

The chief criticism of the scholastic achievement test is not only that it cannot predict the future from past achievement, but also that it cannot measure those educational potentialities that really matter. It does not measure imagination, creativeness, originality, intuitiveness, capacity for further intellectual progress, power to synthesize information from many different sources and apply it to one problem, or ability to see many facts in relation to one another. This weakness of the scholastic achievement test is one reason why so many acknowledged geniuses have had poor school records: the achievement test (on which the records are based) is incapable of measuring or recognizing those qualities that constitute genius. It cannot discover even those students who might do well in graduate work. For the undergraduate who has been able to comprehend and to re-

member perfectly, and even to apply to stated problems
what his professors have told him in class, is not necessarily the person who, in graduate school, can work indepen-
dently or do original and significant research.

A good many investigations have shown that the general high school record of a student has the best predictive value, in relation to college success, of all the devices
so far tested. Even this device, however, is so poor that
average correlations are low, and predictions in any individual case may be utterly false. For example, two boys
living in my neighborhood were the same age, grew up
together, attended the same schools, had the same teachers, and entered the same university. One boy was a star
pupil during all his public school career, received the
American Legion award as the outstanding boy in his
junior high school, and was among the highest 15 per
cent of his graduating class of 585 students. The other
boy was never on any honor roll, was in the highest third
of his class, and was lucky to have been accepted by the
particular college which both boys attended. The first
boy was dropped for scholastic failure at the end of his
junior year; the second boy never had the slightest
scholastic difficulty, and had a better-than-average record during his four years of college.

The high school from which these two boys graduated
is included, by a national investigating body, among the
38 best high schools in the nation, and one of the two in
the entire state to be included. I have just correlated the
record of 40 of this school's honor graduates who were
admitted to my own university with our own records of
honor students as indicated by the Dean's List. The
Dean's List names all students each semester who have
made no grade lower than B. The 40 honor graduates

have just finished their junior year at the university, and therefore have had a chance to appear on the Dean's List six times. Here is what actually happened with these highest-ranking students from one of the nation's highest-ranking high schools:

No. of times on Dean's List	No. of students (among 40 honor graduates from high school)
6	4
5	1
4	3
3	1
2	5
1	8
0	18

In other words, 45 per cent of these top-ranking high school graduates have not distinguished themselves scholastically in college.

Of these 40, moreover, 17 who came to my university were among the top 5 per cent of their graduating class of 590, and were listed as "Graduating With Highest Honors." Of these 17 superselect students, five (30 per cent) never did get on our Dean's List, and three (18 per cent) got on during only one semester.

These figures probably prove that, in a broad general way, "superior" high school students tend to do good work in college. But the tendency is so indefinite, and subject to so many exceptions, that it is quite unreliable as a device for predicting the college success of any particular student.

Falsification by Simplification

A decade or two ago the problem of testing intelligence, aptitudes, and personality seemed fairly simple. But today the problem is recognized as being enormously complex and difficult. As an example of what the tester is up against, let me merely list the chapters in a single book, selected at random off the library shelves, on psychological testing. The chapters are "Intelligence Testing," "Tests of Educational Achievement," "Tests of Educational Aptitude," "Measurement of Special Abilities," "Measurement of Basic Interests," "Measurement of Attitudes," "Measurement of Personal Characteristics," "Measurement of Social Characteristics," "Measurement of Artistic Aptitudes," "Measurement of Professional Aptitudes"; then each of these chapters is subdivided into several parts covering tests for more specific elements appearing under the one chapter heading. In addition, several different methods of measuring each of the multitude of items is described and evaluated according to this particular writer's experience and prejudices. But this is not all. Following this array of complex and difficult problems of measurement come long discussions as to the methods of interpreting accumulated data, with talk about "Factorial Validity," "Empirical Validity," "Specific Norms," "Coefficient of Correlation," "Coefficient of Error," Means, Medians, Percentiles, Variates, and so on.

Yale University makes a gesture toward recognizing some of the complexity and difficulty of testing personalities by selecting its freshmen on the basis of a rather comprehensive "battery" of tests including "Verbal Comprehension," "Artificial Language," "Verbal Reasoning," "Quantitative Reasoning," "Mathematical Ingenuity," and "Spatial Visualizing." The Educational Testing Service at

Princeton has a battery consisting of a Psychological Examination testing scholastic aptitude in the "Quantitative" and "Linguistic" fields, tests on expression and comprehension, and tests on general achievement in social studies, natural sciences, and mathematics. All this suggests the intricacy of the science of mental testing, and the folly of trying to come by any simple and easy answers in this field. Yet all the while that the psychologists are demonstrating that human personality is so complex that a lifetime's work will hardly serve to do more than reveal the problems, not the answers, admissions committees are running students through two afternoons of tests, and coming up with emphatic conclusions that involve the student's entire life. When we remember, too, that all these tests do no more than state that certain complex conditions exist at the *present,* we see how incredibly difficult and dangerous it must be to try to project the results of these tests into the future.

Florence L. Goodenough concludes her book on *Mental Testing* (1949) with five pages of unanswered questions concerning the most elemental problems of her specialty, and adds that these questions "represent only an exceedingly small fraction" of the problems remaining to be solved in the science of mental testing. In view of all this, to say nothing of plain logic and empirical experience year after year, the cavalier assumption (of which the admissions committees of most universities are continually guilty) that a few tests taken on a couple of afternoons by hundreds of prospective students may have any accurate predictive value as to the success of any individual student in the university seems absurdly unrealistic.

This does not imply that psychological tests are worthless. On the contrary, they are extremely valuable — for certain purposes. For one thing, they may indeed be useful in helping committees identify those 15 to 20 per cent of applicants who would almost certainly fail in the university. For another thing, they represent one of the most useful and important scientific developments of our time in their effort to *describe* personality, or to *inventory* personal traits.

But description and inventory must not be confused with *evaluation*. By psychological testing we may discover, for example, that a certain person wishes to be socially dominant. Is this good or bad? Obviously, it may, in some cases, lead to that quality of "leadership" which the admissions committees so admire; or, in other cases, it may lead to social uncooperativeness. Or the testers may find that a certain person has a pacific rather than an aggressive nature. Is this good or bad? It all depends on whether the individual is an official moderator in labor relations, say, or a labor leader. Or that the individual is very fond of the opposite sex. Good or bad? Or he has an intuitive rather than a logical nature. Good or bad? Or he is more interested in people than in ideas. Good or bad? Or he thinks in concrete and practical terms rather than in abstract and theoretical. Good or bad? All these characteristics, and a hundred others, may be recognized and described. But they can be *evaluated* only in relation to certain specific situations that may vary from day to day, or even hour to hour. They can hardly be used as criteria by which admissions committees determine whether or not a youth should be admitted to the university.

The youth living two doors down from me was never able to pass tenth-grade English, and therefore never able to graduate from high school. Yet he can listen to the motor of my automobile, tell me what is wrong with it, advise me about what should be done, tell me the best place to go to have it repaired, tell me how much a mechanic should charge for repairing it, and (if necessary) repair it himself, or even rebuild the motor. He would certainly have failed Yale University's entrance examinations on Verbal Comprehension, Artificial Language, and Verbal Reasoning, as well the most elementary tests on scholastic achievement in English. But who would be a better person to take along on a Yale University expedition exploring central Asia — that boy or me? Another young man who grew up next door is so incompetent in the use of words that he still comes over and has me correct, or even write, his important nonprofessional letters for him; yet he is a successful industrial engineer who helps design great industrial plants all over the nation, and makes considerably more money per year than I do. He too would have flunked the Yale tests. As Miss Goodenough says: "The complexity of the problem is readily seen if one considers a single example. At what point on the continuum running from self-confidence to dependence does the optimum fall? . . . It may vary somewhat with sex; it will certainly change with age. Different occupations call for different amounts of it. Too much would be a handicap for some; too little would spell failure for others." This is a single example from hundreds that might be mentioned. Yet the admissions committees who administer and are guided in their selections by such tests act as if the trait existed in a vacuum, or were an absolute without relation to exterior conditions. The whole system is so fantastic that one wonders how intelligent men could have been taken in by it.

Examiners Examined

Certain factors related to the weaknesses of the examiners, not the examined, contribute heavily to making the efficacy of these tests a delusion.

First, it should be remembered that the tests are made out, administered, and evaluated by people who are, or have been, professors of psychology and professors of education. I have already mentioned some of the deficiencies of the professorial mind and character which suggest that professors are not endowed with a God-like capacity to know, understand, and judge with perfect accuracy. Moreover, if you go into practically any university you care to name, and take a vote among the faculty (exclusive of the professors of psychology and of education) as to which are the two weakest faculty groups in the university, you will invariably find the education faculty leading the list, and the psychology faculty following not far behind. In other words, according to a vote of the faculty in general, the professors of education and of psychology are the very professors who are the most poorly qualified in the university to pass judgment on the ability and intelligence of anybody. I hasten to say that this statement is not fair to every single professor of education or of psychology. Furthermore, the vote of the faculty against these professors may show only that the rest of the faculty lack ability and intelligence. Nevertheless, it indicates something of the complexity of the problem: the very standards by which education and psychology professors measure students may be false standards.

This is one reason why it often happens that a person who knows a great deal about a subject often makes low grades on psychological tests in that very subject. Just the other day a professor of biochemistry in a medical college laughingly told me that, on a routine government psychological test that he had been required to take, his lowest grade was in chemistry. Almost any extensive psychological test one examines carefully will have one or two howlers in it. Thus, I have here a test which, in the section on Verbal Reasoning, has a question in which the answer to be chosen is, "All birds have wings." But a young man who was taking the test, and who happened to be something of an ornithologist, lost two points here because he knew that at least one bird, the Apteryx, does *not* have wings. He knew more than the person who made out the test. Here is another test (for Reading Comprehension) which, describing the live oak tree of the South, says that "It remains green all the year round," pictures a leaf and an acorn and a flower, and then tells the student to draw a circle around the picture that shows what the tree retains all the year round. In the first place, the live oak does not "remain green all the year round," but sheds its leaves in the spring; and in the next place the picture represents a red oak leaf, intricately lobed and pointed, whereas a live oak leaf is a simple ovate leaf like a fat willow leaf. How would a student who knew more about live oaks than the examiner go about answering this question?

Another example may be taken from the practice booklet explaining to the prospective student the Yale Educational Aptitude Battery. Under the heading "Verbal Reasoning" occurs this example:

> Most thunderstorms are accompanied by lightning, rain, and a high wind.
> *Conclusion*: There will be high wind with our next thunderstorm.

The subject is asked to tell whether the *Conclusion* is "Necessarily true," "Necessarily false," "Probably true," "Probably false," "Undetermined" — and the correct answer here is said to be "Probably true."

But anyone with the slightest knowledge of meteorology would probably consider the person who framed this question to be quite ill-informed or irrational. For the probability of a wind with a thunderstorm depends not upon simple annual statistics, but on the season of the year, the temperature, the time of day, the point of origin of the thunderstorm, the terrain over which it moves, and much besides. Thus, the correct answer as to what may happen in "our next thunderstorm" will be one thing if the student is taking the examination in April, and another in July, one thing if he is taking it in New Haven, and another in Idaho. Furthermore, a really precise mind would be troubled concerning the exact meaning of the term "high wind"; and a critical mind would laugh at the statement, "Most thunderstorms are accompanied by lightning" since, obviously, there could be no thunder without lightning.

All this may seem farfetched. But students who are expecting some catch question anyhow, who are painfully eager to make a good showing on this all-important examination, and who do not realize the limitations of professors, are extremely likely to wrestle with all such questions in just the manner I have indicated.

Just one more example may show that ill-framed or inaccurate questions such as these are not exceptional. The very next item (after the thunderstorm just mentioned) in the Yale battery is this:

It is known that only five persons have had this book

152

> and it is improbable that four of them would have written these new marginal notes in it.
>
> *Conclusion*: James, the fifth person, wrote these notes.

The booklet does not tell how this *Conclusion* should be marked. But the answer depends on the real meaning of the word "new." Does it mean "latest of all"? How is the student to know? And what does "the fifth person" mean? Does it mean that James was the *last* person to use the book, or the last one on a list of those known to have used the book? And how strong is "improbable"? Does it mean "virtually impossible," as when one says, "It is improbable that the sun will fail to rise tomorrow"? Or does it have a much weaker meaning? For that matter, among the phrases the student is to choose from in describing the *Conclusion*, are "Probably true" and "Undetermined" mutually exclusive? I am sure that I have not the faintest idea what was in the mind of the psychology professor who made up this question, or what answer he would consider correct — and I doubt that many young high school graduates would have a much clearer idea than I.

Yet the student trying to answer any of the questions mentioned in this section might choose the answer the psychology professor considered wrong, lose points, fail of acceptance by the admissions committee, and have the entire structure of his life altered as a result — all because of professorial incompetence.

Unintelligent Intelligence Tests

The very word *intelligence* bears such a bright aura of favorable connotation in our society, and particularly in educational circles, that anything called an *Intelligence*

Test carries great weight with members of university admissions committees. Groping for some certainty in their selection of students, they follow this test as they would the polestar. Yet if it were called by any other name, they would heed it hardly at all. For example, if it were called a Psychological Puzzle (which is what it is), and yielded, instead of an Intelligence Quotient, or I.Q., a Puzzle Quotient, or P.Q., it never would determine the fate of any prospective student.

There is no doubt that these Psychological Puzzles show *something;* but to call that something *intelligence* is going a little too far in an age which values "intelligence" above everything else. That the professors of education and of psychology have been able to attach the label "Intelligence" to their interesting puzzles is one of the outstanding promotional feats in the realm of modern education.

In the rest of this section I should like to discuss these "Intelligence Tests" as they appear to a layman who has seen them in operation, examined them, and thought about them, for a good many years. First, however, I should like to mention, merely in passing, that even the professional educators and psychologists are not unanimously happy over these tests. Here are some of the objections that have been offered at one time or another by various well-qualified psychologists:

(1) The I.Q. is always closely linked with scholastic achievement, is almost certainly a function of the latter, and therefore has doubtful usefulness as anything more than another type of achievement test. (2) The more often a subject takes intelligence tests, the more proficient he becomes, and the higher scores he makes; that is to say, his "intelligence" was not measured right on his

first test. (3) The same student taking the same test on several successive days will make appreciably different grades. (4) The same student taking several different types of intelligence tests provided by different testing organizations will make several appreciably different grades. (5) Intelligence tests are so largely verbal, or based on verbal directions, sometimes quite complicated and obscurely worded, that the nonverbal type of thinker makes low scores, even though he may be highly proficient in most other qualities of mind or character. (6) One student may rate very high in one part of the test and very low in another, whereas a different student will rate neither very high nor very low in any part, yet the two, however dissimilar they are, will win the same I.Q. rating. (7) Students who are most rapid in expressing knowledge or manipulating puzzles are not necessarily the ones with the most knowledge, the highest intellectual potentialities, or the most original minds. (8) Very young persons in rural and in urban areas have approximately the same I.Q.'s, but by the time they are eighteen the former have much lower I.Q.'s than the latter — the inference being that differences are environmental, not hereditary. (9) The I.Q. is calculated from the average chronological age at which so-called mental growth ceases; yet there is wide disagreement as to what this chronological age is — some setting it at 13 3/4 years, others at 14, others at 15, others at 15 2/3, others at 16, others at 18, others at 20, so that a person having an I.Q. of 100 under one scheme would have an I.Q. of less than 70 under another. (10) The external conditions under which the test is taken, or the emotional condition of the subject, may largely determine the result of the test, and this emotional condition may be a result not of any inborn personal traits but of special situations, such as when a boy from a small country school is brought to a great city and made to take the test in impressive university surroundings, or when a boy from a poverty-stricken family knows that his whole career depends on the grade he makes on the test, or when a timid boy has been embarrassed at the very beginning of the test by some gaucherie of his own or some sarcastic remark of the examiner, and so on. Professor Arthur T. Jersild, in his *The Psychology of Adolescence* (1957), writes: "It is difficult to measure the effect of emotional factors on intellectual performance. Yet anyone who has administered mental tests is repeatedly reminded that they might be highly significant in the case of some individuals." In fact, these emotional factors are probably highly significant in the case of a large proportion of individuals.

But despite all these professionally recognized weaknesses of the intelligence test, and its resulting I.Q., admissions committees everywhere let the applicant's recorded I.Q. influence them in deciding whether or not he shall be admitted to the university.

The objections of a layman to allowing himself to be much influenced by these tests are not so much experimental, or statistical, as logical. In the first place, nobody knows what "intelligence" is. My cat knows how to stalk a bird and catch it with her teeth; but I can accomplish no such feat. Am I less intelligent than she? Out of hundreds of automobiles passing my house hourly, she can identify the sound of my automobile motor a block away, and run to the door to meet me when I appear. My wife cannot distinguish the motor of my car from those of the hundreds of other cars. Is she, therefore, less intelligent than my cat? When I was a boy, I knew each member of a flock of a hundred turkeys on my father's farm *by its face*, and I could not understand how adults could be so stupid as to think all the turkeys looked alike. Was I more intelligent than the adults? An Australian bushman set to herding 300 head of cattle cannot count past 10; but if just one of the cattle is missing, he knows it, and knows which one is missing. Is he more intelligent than the owner of the cattle? When one of my sons was nine years old, he could recognize the make and model of every automobile passing in the street; but I could not. Was I less intelligent than he? A neighbor boy cannot pass either English or chemistry in high school, but he has built television sets and a record-player, and can repair my own television and radio sets. Is he intelligent? Or the senior in college who writes poetry publishable in the best magazines in the country, and writes philosophical and critical articles that astonish me by their brilliance, depth, and originality, but who cannot pass freshman mathematics or freshman chemistry — is he intelligent?

What is this thing *intelligence?* Is it, possibly, a construct of the psychologists and educationists who have arbitrarily set up certain standards that appealed to their own type of mind, and then designated as *intelligent* all those people who approximated those standards, and *unintelligent* all those who varied from those standards? Gulliver's Houyhnhnms thought nobody was beautiful unless he walked on all fours and whinnied like a horse.

In the next place, it ought to be obvious to even a child that intelligence, whatever it is, does not lie in a simple up-and-down line that can be marked off like degrees on a thermometer. It has a qualitative dimension as well as a quantitative; that is, it is not like a narrow line running up and down; it must be more like a fan lying flat, with ribs running in many directions, and most of them on the same level. A poet might not pass a test for "Mechanical Ingenuity," and an engineer might do badly with tests for poetic and artistic appreciation, but does that mean that either the poet or the engineer is intellectually superior or inferior to the other? Of course not. Fortunately, some of the psychologists are beginning to realize the folly of rating intelligence by means of a simple arithmetical scale, and are breaking down their "intelligence tests" into many different types which they rate individually, and do not call "intelligence tests." They are recognizing that some "intelligences" are predominantly abstract and some concrete, some verbal and some imagistic, some intuitional and some logical, some manual and some ideational, some oriented to people and some to things, and so on. Any attempt to blend all these differences in the *quality* of intelligences, and to express them as a single *quantitative* number is utterly unrealistic. It would be like dumping wheat, gravel, confetti, iron filings, gold dust, and feathers into a barrel, and then weighing the mixture and pretending that the weight has any significant relation to the value or to the usefulness of the barrel's contents. Nevertheless, high schools and university admissions committees still give "intelligence tests," and still use them to help decide the fates of students.

Related to what has just been said is the fact that even the "batteries" of psychological tests ("College Aptitude Tests") given by many universities end with an overall grade that hardly recognizes the unilaterally gifted student. The admissions committee that places any reliance on these tests automatically excludes this type of student, yet it is the unilaterally gifted person from whom most of the greatest in human achievement has come. Darwin had no discrimination in music or literature; the painter Turner had no verbal acuity or facility; William Butler Yeats was a child in mathematics; John Steinbeck cannot spell . . . the list could go on and on.

One of the worst features of the "intelligence test" is that it does not even attempt to measure those traits of personality that count far more in making a person admirable or successful or useful to his fellow man than does mere so-called *intelligence*. I mean traits like patience, delight in intellectual activity, pride, reluctance to be mastered by any problem, susceptibility to certain types of intellectual or emotional stimulation resulting in what is called "motivation," insight, wisdom, common sense, understanding of others, tact, and so on. There can be no doubt, for example, that Messrs. Goering, Goebbels, Mussolini, and Stalin were men of superior, if not extraordinary, intelligence. But they possessed (or lacked) certain other traits that invalidated every quality of high intelligence that they possessed, and made them monsters. In other words, a high I.Q. (even if it meant anything at all) does not deserve the approbation that our society automatically gives to any person who has it. Many other qualities are a hundred times more important to society and to the individual himself.

In his *Psychology Applied to Life and Work* (1950), H. W. Hepner writes: "Anyone who does vocational counseling of adults is certain to meet individuals who have high intelligence, pleasing personalities, seemingly good habits, and many good character qualities; but who always manage somehow to fail in their vocations. In

contrast with them, other individuals of less intelligence
. . . manage to succeed." Every parent, teacher, and
university professor who has observed young people
carefully for any length of time has noted just such
discrepancies between intellectual potentialities and
actual accomplishment. The world contains far more good
brains than bad; but it is not mere soundness of brain
that counts. It is what people do with their brains.

At a recent social gathering I heard a distinguished
professor declare roundly: "What we want in the university is students with *brains!*" It may be beside the point
to note, in passing, that this was the professor whom a
confidence man had neatly despoiled of several hundred
dollars the previous year, who invested in a certain stock
at $37 and saw the stock fall within two years (while he
held on) to $8, who was notorious on the campus for
antagonizing all the brightest young men in his department and encouraging all the dull ones who flattered him,
who (when there was more to choose between automobiles than at present) could be regularly depended
upon to buy precisely that automobile that gave the
least service for the most money, and who always voted
for the most reactionary political party on the ballot. But
leaving all that aside, I should like to suggest that the
professor should have said: "What we want in the university is students who can *use* whatever brains they have
for the benefit of themselves and of their fellow man."

There is no doubt that the "intelligence test" can help
the examiner identify persons who are feeble-minded,
moronic, or worse, just as there is no doubt that a physical examination can determine whether a hand is de-
formed, partly paralyzed, or functionally undeveloped.

The examiner might even go so far as to say, in very rough and approximate terms, that an injured hand is 75 per cent efficient, or 50 per cent efficient, or some other similar figure that he lights on, for the sake of filling out insurance papers. But if the hand were quite well, quite normal, undeformed, uninjured, and mature, no physical examiner would be foolish enough to try to rate its quality in terms of precise percentages — Physical Quality 97; Physical Quality 89; Physical Quality 110; and so forth. Nor would any physical examiner try to tell whether any normal, undeformed, uninjured, functionally mature hand could be more efficient in picking a pocket or in playing a piano, in choking a victim or in holding a mechanic's wrench, in wielding a sledge hammer or in throwing a forward pass. Any examiner who tried to tell such precise things would be laughed at.

The brain of a human being is a thousand times more delicate and complex than the human hand. Yet professors of psychology have no hesitancy in rating its quality in precise mathematical terms — I.Q. 130; I.Q. 79; I.Q. 100; and so on — all on the basis of an examination covering an hour or so, worked out with a metallic pencil, and run through an IBM machine. How this absurdity could have become a part of our educational system is one of the mysteries of this century. To be sure, the psychologists will protest that they never meant their tests to be anything more than descriptive; yet the tests are used for other than descriptive purposes. They are used for evaluation, judgment, praise, condemnation. Nor do the psychologists object very strenuously when they see them so used.

The tests help produce a picture of the kind of individual being examined. But putting a precise arithmetical value on this picture, and on the individual, is something very different.

So far in this section I have discussed "intelligence tests" from the point of view of common sense. Statistics could be cited endlessly to substantiate what common sense indicates. For example, I have already mentioned the complete lack of correlation between psychological-test grades and colleges grades among 400 freshmen at my own university, and similar negative results among graduates of Hunter College. In an entire book on *The Failing Student* (1939), Heaton and Weedon examined the records of 983 failing students in four colleges in relation to the grades of these students on the American Council Psychological Examinations. It was discovered that, of all these failing students, only 38 per cent were in the lowest fourth of those taking the psychological examination. If the examinations were accurate predictive instruments, almost 100 per cent of the failures would have occurred in that lowest fourth. Moreover, one third of the failures occurred in the upper half of the students, as ranked by the psychological examination; that is to say, one third of the failures occurred among students ranked above average in relation to national scores. More recently (1955), R. M. W. Travers summarized the conclusions to be arrived at from many investigations of college success in relation to psychological tests. In substance, intelligence quotients "for practical purposes are of only small value for predicting academic achievement in college." Instead, "Motivational factors probably play a major role in determining academic success." And "educational counselors have tended to underestimate these nonintellectual factors and too often have placed excessive reliance on standard measures of scholastic aptitude." Just to complete the picture, all efforts to measure "motivational factors" in relation to college success have produced a correlation "close to zero."*

In concluding this chapter, I should like to make it clear that "intelligence tests" may help admissions committees eliminate that very small percentage of students who have managed to graduate from high school because they were children of leading citizens, or were star athletes, or were problem cases that the high schools graduated just to be rid of them. But it is certain that this group of high school graduates amounts to only a very tiny per cent of the total, so small as to be hardly worth the time, trouble, and expense involved in elaborate testing, especially since the admissions committees are so largely mistaken in their choices in any event.

It should be remembered, too, that there is no way to prove that the rejected students would have done badly if they had been admitted. All we know is that those admitted as a result of the elaborate testing devices are not unqualified successes. From this knowledge, it seems as if we might do well to revise radically our criteria for admission.

In many years of watching the results of admissions

---

* The relation of I. Q. to success in life depends upon the definition of "success." But a study of the careers of 2423 former high school students in Kansas showed that the "professional" class (physicians, lawyers, architects, journalists, professors, teachers, etc.) was almost equally divided among persons of low I. Q., average I. Q., and high I. Q. The figures were these: 32.6 per cent with I. Q. from 75 to 94; 34 per cent with I. Q. from 95 to 105; 33. 4 per cent with I. Q. above 105. (See *American Sociological Review*, 1938, Vol. 3, p. 688.)

committees' work in a university having rather celebrated "high standards" of admission by tests, examinations, and high school records, I have reached this conclusion: If all high school graduates applying for admission were asked to write a short paper, and if this paper proved coherent (not merely "correct"); if all those who wrote coherent papers were interviewed to exclude those who really do not care about going to college, but want to get married, join the army, go to work, or attend a different university; if all were interviewed to exclude those who would labor under a serious financial strain in attending the university; if all those remaining were placed in a large hall; if a handful of peas were cast indiscriminately over the group; and if every person struck by a pea were forthwith admitted to the university, the overall results, measured by success or failure in college courses, would not differ significantly from those obtained by the hard, expensive, and self-sacrificing labors of the admissions committee. This conclusion may be wrong. But I started my teaching career believing in the complete efficacy of the testing and examining system used by the admissions committee, and arrived at this conclusion slowly, and only after thirty years of observing results in my own university, and studying statistics from innumerable sources.

CHAPTER EIGHT

FACING THE MUSIC

Basic Bewilderments

In matters of science and scholarship, the universities are vividly alive to realities. In matters of education they are, as a rule, timid, indecisive, unrealistic, and backward.

For example, practically every one of the most basic problems and most elemental values involved in higher education are now a matter of dispute, indefiniteness, or indifference within the universities. I cannot hope to name all these problems and values about which university people have not made up their minds. But here are ten essential representative questions (chosen almost at random from fifty like them), no one of which has been definitely answered by the universities, or even thought about more than casually by most professors and administrators:

Is college only for the intellectually elite?
> OR *Does every boy and girl in America have an inalienable right to higher education?*

Is college only for those who will become the leaders of our society?

OR *Is college for those who are certain to be followers and inferiors in our society?*

Is college education, which is paid for by society, meant primarily to prepare students to serve society more efficiently?

OR *Is college education meant primarily for the welfare (financial, intellectual, spiritual) of the individual?*

Can society afford to pay for the higher education of every Jack and Jill in the nation?

OR *Can society afford not to pay for the higher education of every Jack and Jill in the nation?*

Should the colleges "maintain their standards" so that, even if all young people have an opportunity to enter college, a very large number are dropped?

OR *Should colleges "lower their standards" so that all young people who enter college may obtain some-thing of value from their college experience?*

Should college try to establish in the student's mind the rightness of the political and economic system that enables him to go to college?

OR *Should college try to make the student question and examine our present economic and political system, with a view to improving it, or even discarding it, if any other system seems "better"?*

Is college meant to confirm the student in orthodox Judaeo-Christian religious beliefs?

OR *Is college meant to encourage the student to question all his inherited religious beliefs, and even to discard them if he finds them personally unsatisfactory?*

Does the chief responsibility of the student's getting a college education lie within himself?

> OR *Does the chief responsibility for the student's getting a college education lie partly, or largely, with his professors?*

Is college meant primarily to prepare the student for a successful professional career?

> OR *Is college meant primarily to make the student an intrinsically worthwhile person, according to the highest standards of our civilization?*

Should the college aim chiefly at providing the student with information, knowledge of nature's laws, knowledge of society's laws, and methods by which the student may discover more information and learn more laws?

> OR *Should the college aim chiefly at creating in the student certain attitudes of mind, certain interests, certain intellectual habits, certain intellectual objectives, certain fundamental values which he considers more important than anything else in his life?*

All these sample questions are absolutely basic . . . yet the universities have not faced up to answering any of them. Perhaps that is a major reason why higher education is, by and large, so unsuccessful. "It can be established as an educational law," says President Upton of Beloit, "that education in the fullest sense of the word cannot materialize without a definite idea of what the end product is to be." But, as a rule, neither professors, nor students, nor administration in the American university have decided "what the end product is to be." Meanwhile, the university remains, for most students, the place where you accumulate enough credits to pay for a diploma and a degree, get a sorority or a fraternity pin, attend some happy student social affairs, see some football games, acquire a certain self-confident air that distinguishes you from the noncollege person, and helps you in business, and maybe meet the girl or the man you will marry.

Perhaps the universities should face up to reality at last, and try to decide just what they are trying to accomplish. It is imperative that they make that decision *now,* for it seems likely that most American universities are going to acquire an increasingly uniform pattern. Already the old-time independent colleges, each with its own objectives, are being replaced by, or overshadowed by, or influenced by, great interlocking systems of state colleges and universities, all with uniform requirements and methods, or by three or four great private universities (Harvard, Yale, Princeton, Chicago) which themselves set the pattern for one another and for many of the state systems. All these colleges and universities supply one another with professors, transfer students from one to the other, have the same roster of courses and credits, borrow books from one another's libraries, send professors to conventions on one another's campuses, and continually hold conferences in which they share one another's views on the problems of higher education.

As the colleges and universities grow bigger, and more important in the nation's life, as they will certainly do in the coming decades, it seems likely that, instead of becoming less uniform, they will become more uniform. It is characteristic of bigness to promote uniformity. Besides, as the government (state or Federal) gives more and more aid to higher education, as it will certainly have to do in the years ahead, the uniformity is bound to increase still further. The government will name conditions under which colleges and universities will receive government aid, and these conditions will have to be uniform for most of the country.

The probability that, in the decades just ahead, we shall see a single set of educational ideals blanketing the nation is the chief reason why everybody concerned with higher education, or likely to be concerned with it in the future, should face up to the issues and try to determine what the aims of higher education should be. If we wait much longer, we shall find that we have missed the boat. Our system of higher education will have become too enormous, too firmly entrenched in law and custom, too monolithic, to be affected ever again by bold formulative ideals.

We must try to find and adopt *now* for our colleges and universities some permanently seminal principles, some vision that contains infinite possibilities of unfolding change, some ideals that will be as sound several centuries from now as they are today, some basic doctrines that will hold men and at the same time liberate men. Unless we can do this *now*, our system of higher education may develop into the same sort of intellectual and moral slavishness that has characterized fascist and communist higher education in this century, or into some atrophied, scholastic mandarinism, devitalizing and dangerous.

Trumpet-Calls Unheeded

Another fact that the universities are going to have to face up to very soon is that the whole moral temper of this age is different from that of the age just past; that mental attitudes expected of young people fifty years ago are nonexistent today; that patterns of behavior universal then are nowhere to be found today; that "ideals by which men lived" then are dead today; that appeals to elements of character that were effective then only create a laugh now; and that incentives that meant everything then are impotent now. Perhaps all is not as it *should* be; at any rate, a good many older people are objecting to it. But it is a condition that exists, nevertheless, and must be recognized. Perhaps it is not even necessary to regret it. Generations are always changing; older people are always regretting; and today's younger people seem to be doing no worse a job with the world than the older people did in their day. At any rate, one thing is sure: the universities, with their long traditions and their business of transmitting to youth the heritage of the past, are not adapting themselves very rapidly to the new conditions. Until they face this fact, they will not be ready to launch themselves on a new career of effective teaching.

To outline the changes that have taken place in the moral tempers, mental attitudes, behavior, ideals, and character of young people in the last forty or fifty years would require a book several times the length of this one. But certain of the most significant changes can be briefly suggested.

The change in the attitude toward sex is one of the most obvious, and one with the most far-reaching implications. What was formerly seldom mentioned or hardly acknowledged in ordinary society, what was hidden inside oneself with a sense of guilt, is now recognized openly as, probably, the most important element in personality. Sex calls to us from periodical advertisements and from billboards, from movies and television, from stories and novels, from psychiatrists' offices and popular articles in magazines and newspapers, from the dresses of women and the conversation of men — everywhere.

This change in the general attitude toward sex has changed the entire concept of marriage from a hard duty and a heavy responsibility to a pleasure. And when it is no longer a pleasure, it is shuffled off in the thriving divorce courts. This change has created a certain sense of equality and "togetherness" in the marriage relationship nowadays; no longer do we think of the dominating and lordly husband and father paired off with the meek and humble wife and mother. Both husband and wife have become more human, more natural, less patriarchal or matriarchal, less a supreme authority ruling by divine right.

This change in the relationship of married couples has altered the entire tone and temper of family life. The ideals of duty and responsiblity in the marriage relationship have been replaced almost everywhere by the value of pleasure and delight. Pleasure recognized as the most fundamental element in the most fundamental of instincts carries over into other relationships, coloring them all. This generation is bent on getting as much joy as possible out of life; and never was there a generation that offered more opportunities for people to have joy. Marriage has become a pleasure, not a duty; children are a pleasure, not a duty; church attendance must be made a pleasure, not a duty, if the minister expects the pews to be filled; every counselor of youth advises, "First of all, find a work in which you can be reasonably happy," not, "First find where your duty lies, and then do it"; every employer must make conditions of work as enjoyable as possible if he expects to keep his employees — he must provide coffee breaks, air-conditioning, shorter hours, company picnics, agreeable surroundings, office parties, vacations, retirement pensions, congeniality —

he would not get far by merely holding up to his employees the ideals of duty and hard work. Furthermore, Americans everywhere are making every effort to devise and utilize thousands of labor-saving devices from can openers to monstrous cranes; drinking for pleasure is universal; foods are packaged and displayed to please the eye and tempt the palate; automobiles are sold not so much by the efficiency of their motors as by the luxury of their appointments. Finally, it is pretty obvious that the people in our society who work the hardest (ditch-diggers, farmers, common laborers) are seldom the ones who get the most wealth, comfort, and joy out of life.

Well, under these circumstances, just what results do the educators expect to get when they blare out their trumpet-calls to abstract duty and hard work as ideals for modern university students? Perhaps the students *should* follow after those ideals. But they *don't*. Refusal to face this perfectly obvious fact, and to adjust to it, is one reason why the universities fail so badly with so many of their students.

The change in the relationship of husband and wife has likewise effected a change in the relationship of parent and child. The father who tries, by stern parental discipline or by an implied appeal to the divine right of parents, to control his children, or to make them aspire toward the kind of life he thinks is good for them — "Do this because I say so, and because God commands you to honor your father and your mother" — will not get very far with his children. He has to appeal to them on the basis of reason, affection, and the well-being of the entire household. He has to meet his child at least halfway, listen to the young person's reasons for doing things, try to see the young person's point of view, and guide the young person on the basis of some sort of reasonable compromise between two views. The parent who tries this method on modern youth will accomplish something. If he lays down the law — "Thou shalt," or "Thou shalt not" — he will produce only delinquents.

Whether we like it or not, young people today have to be persuaded and reasoned with, and even tempted, to do what we think is good for them. (Some people may think it is asking a good deal of a parent to be forever persuading, reasoning with, and tempting a child to do what the parent knows is good for the child; but it is considerably less disturbing, less wearing, more loving, and more effective than beating.) Today's university students have never acquired the habit of automatically and mechanically obeying arbitrary orders: "Learn this, learn that. Take this course because I say it's good for you. Follow this educational program because I tell you to." It would be much easier for the professors if the students would go along enthusiastically with such a discipline. On the other hand, it is doubtful whether students who have become smoothly working automata responding automatically to the command of their masters constitute the perfect ideal which a democratic culture that values the dignity of the individual is trying to attain. The professors really know this; they are continually demanding that students *think*. But, with characteristic schizophrenia, they are continually demanding discipline and self-discipline (where *self-discipline* means doing exactly what the professors say). The universities had better face up to this schizophrenia. They had better realize that they cannot produce well-disciplined students and at the same time produce independent-minded, self-respecting, original, courageous, and intrinsically worth-while human beings.

The entire family background of the modern American student makes it impossible for him to be a well-disciplined automaton. The efforts of the university to uniformize and discipline him with required courses, required credits, required grades, required work, in which he has not been able to see the sense, may result in his making a gesture toward meeting the requirements, since he has no choice in the matter if he is to stay in the university. But the gesture will be halfhearted and perfunctory at best, and stubbornly resentful at worst, with the result that all the fine structure of requirements, planned so carefully by the university authorities to give the student the education that they think he needs, will result in the usual uninspired and reluctant student who becomes the usual half-failure. The trumpet-calls of duty, of hard and disagreeable work, of rigid discipline, no longer rouse our young people. Some professors may think it a pity; but what they think cannot alter the fact. And perhaps it is not a pity, after all. Perhaps the trumpet-calls of reason, affection, independence, self-determination, self-reliance, originality, and love of learning are as worthy of being heeded as were the older trumpet-calls.

Mistrustful Students

Another thing the universities might do well to face up to is the fact that young people no longer feel that they are living in a stable world of established values. They have not been born into a world where all the answers to all the problems are already known, where right and reason have clearly established themselves, where truth

is universally recognized and permanently fixed in the pre-
vailing culture, where, in the words of George Meredith,
it is the first evidence of sanity "to believe that our
civilization is founded in common sense," and where,
in the words of Robert Browning, "All's right with the
world." Young people do not have to be preternaturally
clever to perceive that a world living under the shadow
of the mushroom cloud is not precisely a success; that a
world living (if the pundits are correct) on the peak of
inflation and on the brink of another depression that may
"curl your hair" is not precisely stable; that a world
divided between angry hundreds of millions proclaiming
that one way of life is the ideal, and other hundreds of
millions proclaiming that another way of life is the ideal,
cannot have reached any permanent solution to its most
elemental questions. When these young people come to
the university and find that not even the professors have
answered the most elemental questions about society at
large (or even about society in little, the university itself),
how can these young people feel that any ideal presented
to them is true, stable, and trustworthy? If they are a little
averse to learning exactly what they are told, a little
skeptical about the educational programs laid out for
them, a little cynical about the alleged truths that the
professors try to teach them, a little unconcerned with
learning truths that they suspect are only half-truths and
temporary truths and convenient truths and no truths —
who can blame them, and who is to blame? More important still, how are the universities going to teach them?
Shall the universities have no devices more imaginative,
more convincing, and more realistic than the old admo-
nitions: "Work hard. Do your duty. Your elders know best.
Learn what we say is the truth. Do not doubt us. Just

put your nose to the grindstone and learn what you are told to learn." The modern university student simply will not grow enthusiastic over such an approach. Perhaps he should; but he won't. Yet the universities keep refusing to face this fact, and keep relying on an educational approach that has not been really efficient since 1910.

Education by Punishment

This brings up the complex problem of *motivation*.

The universities have hardly been facing up to the problem of student motivation in the modern world. Instead, the universities have been expecting the old motivations to continue to be effective. In the past, the universities have commanded: "Learn this!" and students in the past have learned. They learned for several reasons, some of which may be worth a glance here just to show that they no longer characterize the society in which we live.

First, in the old days, when relatively few people went to college, the young man (it was nearly always a man) in college felt himself to be a somewhat unique and privileged being; this feeling of dignity and self-importance was enough of itself to make him eager to "take advantage of his opportunities" in college. Second, he was living in an era when truths about the most important things (religion, morality, government, economics, society, art) were well known, well established, and seemingly permanent; obviously he had to learn these obvious truths if he expected to have even the rudiments of an education. Third, in the midst of a world generally noneducated, he had a touching, almost religious dedication to "getting an education"; it was like seeking salvation, it was a moral duty, it was a kind of Protestant responsibility. Fourth, his going off to the university often entailed a major financial sacrifice by his honored parents; for their sake he *had* to make good. Fifth, he lived in a kind of masochistic time when (in England and in America) people felt instinctively that whatever was unpleasant was good and desirable — that castor oil and Epsom salts were much better for everybody than the despised "sugar-coated pill" — and the very fact that learning was disagreeable work made it good and desirable. Finally, he had a sense of duty that, undoubtedly, was far sterner than the sense of duty in today's university student.

All of these motivations in higher education are either absent or badly faded today. We may wish it were otherwise; but wishing does not alter the fact.

Motivations may be, and have been, classified in many ways. For present purposes it may be sufficient to classify them as *positive* or *negative*. That is, some motivations may lead an individual toward a pleasant and desired goal; and others may urge him away from an unpleasant and undesired experience. I shall consider *negative motivation* first.

It is true that people may learn under threat of punishment. But nobody learns gladly through this process; few people learn eagerly any more than is necessary to escape punishment; it almost inevitably makes people hate education thus associated with punishment; and it tends to make everybody forget the whole painful experience of education-linked-to-punishment. Moreover, where learning is achieved chiefly through threat of punishment, the relation between student and master must be that of enemies. This state of warfare (universal, seemingly, in schools of the nineteenth century) makes life miserable for all concerned, and accomplishes a minimum of education. The only reason that it worked in past years was that it was reinforced by the universal conviction that the schoolmaster was pounding absolute "truths" into the bottoms of the pupils, and also by a universal awe for the stern authority of Scripture which had got itself related to the educational process. Since both these elements are lacking in modern education, the old-fashioned pounding on bottoms has proved ineffective, and has gradually been abandoned.

In our better elementary and junior high schools, the place of the old-time savage teacher with his bundle of rods has been taken by the child psychologist, child guidance clinics, counselors, parent-teacher conferences, and a general effort to make school more pleasant for the children. That is, the shift has been away from negative motivation toward positive motivation. Of course, much of this development has been bitterly opposed by a certain percentage of the older generation who, still steeped in the thinking of the nineteenth century, grumble continually because the schools have been made more pleasant for children. They think that a school is not a school unless it makes pupils miserable.

The universities, however, still rely very largely on this negative motivation, a fear of external punishment, as a means of persuading students to learn. There is the ever-present threat of dropping the student from the rolls of the university. (Nobody seems to realize that dropping a student does not actually solve the problem; it only gets rid of the problem here and now, and creates much more difficult and complicated problems hereafter. Kicking a student out may be convenient, but it is not educating him. Every student kicked out is another failure for the university.) Other external punishments which the universities threaten include putting a student "on probation," depriving him of certain campus privileges, withholding certain credits and degrees, and (above everything else) giving him a bad grade. The result is that the vast majority of students work for grades alone. They want to escape this rather humiliating form of punishment. They develop no positive love for the courses they are taking or the learning they are acquiring; they have not the slightest compunction in registering for a conveniently scheduled course in which they have no interest, receiving a grade in it, getting a credit, and then forgetting immediately everything they have learned in the course. Some of them have no compunction about cheating in order to get a grade; most of them do as little work as possible in order to win as high a grade as possible. The emphasis is everywhere distorted. And the students are not to blame. The university's intricate rules, regulations, and requirements are centered about grades; the professors grow deadly serious over the matter of grades; the students are almost never informed that anything matters except the grades. The university should face the fact that all these efforts to motivate the student to learn are negative, and that they belong to the nineteenth century, not the twentieth.

A second kind of negative motivation involves self-punishment (adminstered from within) instead of external punishment (administered from without) which we have just been discussing. Self-punishment consists in the subject's forcing himself, without external compulsion, to do something unpleasant. We generally describe this sort of punishment as "answering the call of duty."

The problem of duty is extremely complex. In the nineteenth century Robert E. Lee declared: "Duty is the sublimest word in our language." But in the twentieth century the novelist Norman Douglas has said, "When duty ceases to be a pleasure, then it ceases to exist." The two aphorisms seem to contradict each other; but perhaps they are more nearly identical than would appear. With acute psychological insight, Mark Twain once wrote: "Duties are not performed for duty's sake, but because their neglect would make the man uncomfortable." That is to say, an individual would suffer more by not doing his duty than by doing it. His doing his duty, therefore, is an attempt to escape the inner punishment that he would inflict on himself if he did not do it. For example, a father may not enjoy crawling out of a warm bed on a winter night to go see if his children are snugly covered against the cold; but if he remained in bed, his conscience would punish him so severely that he could not go back to sleep or rest easy for the remainder of the night. Therefore, he chooses the lesser punishment, and gets up. The decision to do one's duty is sometimes hard to make; that is because it is sometimes hard for one to decide which course of action will bring the least self-punishment. In any event, doing an unpleasant duty is negatively motivated action; it is an attempt to escape from an even more unpleasant experience.

A sense of duty driving a student to engage in disagreeable study might involve certain lifelong habits of study, breaking which would be extremely unpleasant to the student; or it might involve a desire not to incur parental reprimand, or even parental disappointment; it might involve desire to excel, or self-respect, or moral values, and so on. All this presupposes, however, that studying is unpleasant. It involves negative motivation — an urge to escape from an unpleasant and undesired inner experience. Another name for this self-punishment for the sake of escaping a more severe self-punishment is *self-discipline*.

This type of motivation is not officially recognized. But most parents, most professors, and most university administrations spend a great deal of time appealing solemnly to the student's sense of duty, or trying hopelessly to graft a sense of duty into his personality. In the present state of our culture, with the tags of masochistic Puritanism-Victorianism still clinging to us, appeals to a student's sense of duty, to his powers of self-discipline, are sometimes effective. But we ought to face up to the fact that this appeal to duty has several things wrong with it.

First, it is always our own notions (as parents or professors) about duty, and not the student's, that we try to appeal to or develop in the student("Duty is what one expects of others," said Oscar Wilde). Second, the appeal works in only a small percentage of students. And third, the entire assumption that it is the student's *duty* to study implies that studying is a disagreeable necessity. When, in appealing to a student's sense of duty, we say, "You must put more time on your work," we really mean, "You are not making yourself sufficiently miserable." When we tell him, "You must study harder," we really mean, "Don't try to get any fun out of your studies." When we tell him, "You must learn to pay stricter attention to business," we really mean, "See that you don't enjoy getting an education."

If this type of negative motivation really worked with most students, something might be said for it. But, as I have tried to point out in another chapter, it works very poorly. By far the larger part of university graduates carry over into their postuniversity life virtually none of the intellectual interests, activities, and values that (supposedly) occupied them for four years in the university. The only exceptions to this rule are the technological students (engineers, chemists, pharmacists, etc.); these do carry away something that serves them later. But, as will be seen immediately, these students were positively, not negatively, motivated in the university. Most university graduates turn out to be failures, or almost failures, in nearly every category in which the university has tried to educate them through negative motivation.

Education by Delight

Positive motivation may be subdivided into two types: motivation for reward, and motivation by delight.

Motivation for reward is the urge, or the willingness, to perform an action for the sake of some completely unrelated reward. Thus, a trained seal eagerly balances balls and plays trumpets, not for the joy of balancing and playing, but for the fish with which he will be rewarded.

Universities unblushingly make use of this sort of motivation in order to persuade students to study. They offer rewards in good grades, credits, and degrees — none of them any more related to learning and to education than a fish is related to playing a trumpet. Mindful of Napoleon's remark, "We manage men with toys," the universities offer the rewards of "Dean's List," Phi Beta Kappa keys, and graduation *cum laude*. I will not pause to examine the way in which the prospect of these goodies makes students take easy courses in which they are sure to get high grades, or creates bitter feeling toward professors who do not give expected high grades, or stirs up jealousies among students, or makes learning a nightmare of drudgery, or breaks hearts, or instills a gnawing sense of inferiority, or causes harsh recrimination from parents whose egos are disappointed, or encourages hatred for the university and for education itself. All I want to do is suggest the sadly mistaken and distorted values involved in the manner in which the universities dangle these rewards.

Less tinsely are the rewards offered to graduates of the technical and professional schools — monetary rewards. Because our culture values financial success so highly, and because technical or professional education promises financial success, most students will work diligently to perfect themselves in these fields, even though they may have little liking or aptitude. The alluring monetary reward, with its accompanying social prestige, is sufficient motivation for their studying.

On the other hand, it should be said that some of the universities are beginning to ask their prospective engineers, chemists, lawyers, physicians, and physicists some detailed questions about whether they would really enjoy, or could be taught to enjoy, the profession they intend to enter. And many students are asking themselves the same questions. "Job satisfaction" and "contentment with career," that is, enjoyment of the prospective work, seem to be more important considerations today than they have ever been before. Nevertheless, it must be said that the great majority of universities still merely take the student's word for what he feels inclined to study as a profession, and run him through the necessary courses. Since, however, not one eighteen-year-old youth in a hundred knows what his real likes and abilities are, a great many misfits result. Early in this century, the misfitted student would feel duty-bound to continue with his career, even if he hated it. Today the prospective rewards of money and social prestige hold him in line. Yet both the call of duty and the call of money and prestige are sounding fainter and fainter in the ears of this generation of students who have learned to think that life should be enjoyed. Accordingly, many of these youngsters in the technical and professional schools are likely to become failing, disinterested, mediocre students who change their majors by the hundreds, or develop feelings of frustration and unsuccess, sullen resentment against the educational system, humiliation, and disillusionment, often resulting in withdrawal from college.

The Soviet Union has apparently been able to incite its students to intensive work by doubly motivating them — with promised rewards of money and social prestige, and also by inculcating them with a kind of dedicated patriotism not unlike the Puritan-Victorian urge toward duty, self-discipline, and self-punishment that prevailed in America at the beginning of this century.

For the few months intervening between the launching of the Russian *sputniks* and our own, it seemed as if a dedicated spirit, similar to that existing in Russia, entered our students. But at the present writing that spirit has waned, and the universities, despite all the public clamor caused by the realization that all Russians were not peasants, seem to have returned to their pre-*sputnik* inadequacies.

It is astonishing in view of our general democratic emphasis on a good life for the individual citizen, and of our twentieth-century preoccupation with making life as pleasant, happy, and enjoyable as possible, that we should not have tried to show our college students that studying may constitute a good life, and be a pleasant, happy, and enjoyable occupation. But practically nobody in any uni-

versity I know about has taken this obvious, but revolu-
tionary, step. We are still acting as if studying were a
highly unpleasant necessity, still trying to persuade people
to study by the lure of campus honors and post-graduate
money and prestige, and still insisting that the student
keep his nose to the grindstone out of a sense of duty.

My own strong belief is that the one really priceless
contribution a university can make to the student as an
individual, and to the nation at large, is to show him that
there is delight in learning, to indicate to him the
continents of learning in which he can discover delight,
to make him itch to explore those continents, and to give
him the equipment with which he can do his exploring.
"No work can be counted really good," says Masefield,
"till it uses the lively and lovely qualities of the worker."

In the elementary school and, to a certain extent, in
the junior high school, teachers and pupils alike have
learned, in Yeats' words, that

> Wisdom is a butterfly,
> And not a gloomy bird of prey.

But suddenly, in high school and in college, the student
becomes "responsible," and is expected to inflict self-
punishment, to develop a sense of duty and to discipline
himself to endure the gloominess of education. *Shades of
the prison-house begin to close/ Upon the growing
Boy.* It is universally assumed that learning has now
become an unpleasant task to which the student must
be driven, or to which he must drive himself. "The tragedy
of American education," said President Gould of Antioch
recently, "appears to be that the initial sense of wonder
and the urge to explore, so characteristic of the young

child, are lost in his secondary schooling and are never rediscovered through his years of higher education. Somewhere along the line a stultifying process takes place."

But I do not believe that this stultifying process is inevitable. The sense of wonder survives with many students who become graduate students, and with a large percentage of students who become professors; and it is sometimes resurrected, long after graduation, in persons who discover some new continent of learning to be explored. I meet these explorers all the time. Some have had four years of a university; some have never seen a university campus. They tell me volumes about native trees and wildlife, about the techniques of painting and sculpture, about boats and automobiles, about novels and poems, about economics and politics. I know a former student who graduated (with mediocre grades) as a mechanical engineer, but who knows more about modern drama than any college professor I ever met; I know one who graduated in chemistry, but is now a national figure in ornithology; I know one who never went to college at all, but has made a national reputation in ichthyology; I know another who never went to college, but knows more about the economics of the stock market than any professor of economics at my university; I know one who got through college on very average grades as a business administration major, but is now an authority on the Confederate Navy. It is not a dreamy and idealistic hope that "the initial sense of wonder and the urge to explore" should be preserved in high school and in college, that students may actually *want* to learn, delight in learning. There is too much evidence in too many people that this delight may continue for a lifetime.

186

President Gould says that this delight is "lost." Perhaps it would be more accurate to say that it is *killed* — by high school teachers and university professors. Why do they kill it, why do they do so little to encourage their students to find a spontaneous joy in learning? Doesn't the answer lie in the lingering influence of the Puritanic-Victorian tradition that learning is a burdensome task, a hard self-discipline, a difficult work that the student can be persuaded to perform only by threat of punishment, exhortation to duty, and promise of rewards?

The truth is that a very great many people, perhaps all people, will work just for the joy of the working. It is unfortunate that the universities make very little attempt to appeal to this fundamental trait of the human character. They should face up to the fact that they are neglecting this type of motivation in trying to get their students to learn, and are appealing instead to fear of punishment, self-discipline, extraneous academic rewards, and monetary inducements. "Learning," says Dean Burchard of M.I.T., "is not admired for its own sake in very many quarters." The universities and the university professors have done very little to try to cultivate this admiration — or, better, this love, this delight — among their students.

Delight versus Duty

As a matter of fact, it sometimes looks as if the universities and the university professors were trying to cultivate just the opposite attitude among their students. In almost any educational journal one picks up, in speeches by commencement orators, in pronouncements by university presidents, we hear that these are "grim times" (by the way, can anyone remember when we were not living in "grim times"?); we hear that studies are "weapons for survival"; we hear that "habits of hard and cheerful work are basic to success in all human endeavors" (which should be good news to the Negro laborers of the South and the Irish laborers of Boston); we hear that the student "should not be permitted to waste time"; and we hear that a university should not be "a place of mere entertainment."

Actually, the ideal university would be a place of "mere entertainment." If students could be taught that learning is at least as pleasant and delightful as playing a rubber of bridge, or watching a commercial-sprinkled television program, or going to a third-rate movie, or seeing some hulking boys running this way and that way with a football, we should have no educational problems whatever. If we could somehow get over to all the students (as we do get over to 10 to 15 per cent of them) that learning is the finest entertainment in the world — the most absorbing, the most enduring, the most intoxicating, the most irresistible, the most completely satisfying — we should have very little worrying to do about these "grim times." The Athenians were, for a while, able to see learning as entertainment, and during that time accomplished what has echoed through twenty-five centuries. Some Italians, Frenchmen, and Englishmen accomplished it during the Renaissance. "In my study," says one of those men of the Renaissance, Machiavelli, "I feel no weariness, I forget every trouble, poverty does not dismay me, death does not terrify me." And many a scientist and scholar these days (even the ones who tell their students that learning is hard work, painful duty, and rigor-

ous self-discipline, not "mere entertainment") find infinite delight in learning. Their wives will be the first to
testify that not even the lure of meals, of social intercourse, of theatre or stadium, will draw them, except reluctantly, from the delight of their books, their library, or
their laboratory. "The same thrill," says Professor Feyn-
man, of Caltech, "the same awe and mystery, come again
and again when we look at any problem deeply enough.
With more knowledge comes deeper, more wonderful
mystery, luring one to penetrate deeper still." John Ruskin
put it this way: "The entire object of true education is to
make men not merely do the right things, but enjoy the
right things." Perhaps if the university professors would
try to impart to their students a thrill, a delight, an enjoyment in learning, they would not have to be calling
them so often (and so futilely) to remember duty.

The whole problem of teaching successfully is solved
as soon as the student perceives that there is delight in
learning; or rather, as soon as he perceives that learning is
not hard work, painful duty, and rigorous self-discipline.
Being a primate, he has in his blood an itching curiosity,
an urge to monkey about, an irresistible inclination to ape
what he sees in the world. The task of the teacher amounts
to hardly more than allowing these traits of this interesting primate to have full sway, and to suggest places
where he can exercise them. "If you insist upon teaching
a child," says Bertrand Russell, "he will conclude that he
is being asked to do something disagreeable to please you,
and he will have a psychological resistance . . . . If, on
the contrary, you can first stimulate the child's desire to
know, and then, as a favor, give him the knowledge he
wants, the whole situation is different . . . . But if external authority is necessary to induce a boy or a girl to learn,

unless there is a medical cause, the probability is that the teacher is at fault."

Here is the nub of this book. Students in our universities are *not* learning as they should; and the teacher *is* at fault.

It is hard to have patience any longer with the "sense of duty" in higher education. There is a kind of mind which says: "I read Shakespeare, and listen to Beethoven, and learn about the Greeks, and try to understand the basic principles of evolution or of atomic physics only because it is my painful duty to do so in these grim times." What a loathsome reason for doing those things! This is the kind of person who would say, "I eat only because it is my duty to retain my health," or "I kiss my wife only because it is my duty as a twentieth-century American husband," or "I see that my children are fed only because it is my duty as a respectable father," or "I help the unfortunate only because it is my duty as a Christian." In each case this person does the right thing, but does it for a completely reprehensible reason.

A great deal may be said, after all, for Dr. Peale's "positive thinking." One should eat because he loves good food; he should kiss his wife because he loves her; he should feed his children because he loves them; he should help the unfortunate because he loves his fellow man. And he should learn because he loves learning.

The only person more loathsome than the duty-addict is the one who says, "I read Shakespeare, and listen to Beethoven, and learn about the Greeks, and try to understand the basic principles of evolution and of atomic physics — and I kiss my wife and feed my children and help my neighbor — only because, later on, I shall somehow manage to convert all this into cash."

190

Let us face the fact: the universities have done a great deal to encourage, and very little to discourage, these two types of loathsomeness.

The Blight of the University

One more aspect of motivation for the university student must be mentioned. It is *anti-motivation*, or *reverse motivation*. It is the psychological characteristic (suggested by Russell in the passage quoted above) that neither drives a person nor lures a person in the direction we should like to have him go, but causes him to go in the opposite direction.

In a recent article of great perceptiveness, John R. Anderson, of Virginia Polytechnic Institute, points up this problem of reverse-motivation: "Many unsuccessful students are potentially capable, but have failed to apply themselves effectively. Most observers are in agreement that the problem has to do with the question of motivation, but some college officials have assumed that this means *lack* of motivation." But, Professor Anderson goes on to say, these students probably do not suffer from "deficient motivation"; rather, "it may be assumed that students who have not applied themselves do not lack motivation but probably have unconscious negative attitudes that predispose them to failure . . . unseen negative motives are sabotaging the efforts and ambitions of the individual."

This "tendency toward self-sabotage" may rise from a deep unconscious antagonism toward one or both parents because of their attempt to dominate the student's life and career. Or it may rise from the student's feeling that his parents do not love him enough, or have intelligence enough to understand his problems at the university. Or the parents' extreme preoccupation with the student's making good grades, their "excessive exhortation to excel," their putting the student under false pressures, may have motivated the student not to try to learn but to try to make good grades, regardless of learning.

Thus far Professor Anderson. But he does not say that a student who is highly original and imaginative may (consciously or unconsciously) so resent the elaborate network of university requirements, the channeled programs that he must follow, the delightful courses that he is forbidden to take, the credits in this or that doleful minor that he must rack up, the dreary and pedestrian assignments that he is forced to complete, the memorizing of details that he must do in preparation for examinations (and that he will have forgotten a week after he takes the examination), the cut-and-dried lectures that he must listen to, the discouragement of original approaches to problems that the professors know have already been satisfactorily solved in other ways, the punishment in bad grades for irreverence toward the private gods whom the professor worships — the original and imaginative student may so resent all this that he is motivated *not* to learn.

Or perhaps the student was brought up in a cultured and gentle environment where good manners were practiced, and consideration was evinced for other people, and minds were sensitive to courtesy and thoughtfulness. When a student like this meets an intellectually arrogant professor with a domineering manner and a boorish disregard for personal feelings, how can the student help curling up inside a shell of resentment, hating the professor and all he stands for, and resolving never to study in that man's course again?

Or perhaps the student comes from some small high school whose congenial teachers recognized him as a person, understood his abilities, and gave him a sense of delight in learning. He is thrown into a university world where he is "processed" by an IBM machine, overwhelmed with "required" courses, shunted about as impersonally as if he were a freight car (often by subdeputy functionaries who take pride in being as rude as they possibly can), told to "work hard" and to keep his nose to the grindstone, and practically forbidden to take any delight in learning. Well, how can the university officials and professors be shocked and surprised when this student does not learn, and actually seems to resent the university and its dull, stony, well-intentioned offerings?

What a melancholy list of unrealized and frustrated young men — some of them the most brilliant and promising I have ever known — comes to memory after years of teaching experience; young men who left the university in despair before graduation, or remained on in despair just long enough to eke out a degree. They *needed* the university; they *needed* encouragement by more mature minds; they *needed* acquaintanceship with "the best that has been thought and said in the world"; they *needed* companionship with other original and brilliant young minds; they *needed* the orderly development of their talents. Young poets, artists, musicians, critics, dramatists, novelists, philosophers, architects, historians, all subjected to administration requirements: "Conform or be damned!" To professorial requirements: "Conform or be damned!" To student pressures: "Conform or be damned!" And all ruined and damned forever because they could not conform.

Perhaps it is in the antimotivations that they inspire in students that the universities fail most tragically and criminally. But it is hard to decide. There are so many tragedies and so many crimes in our universities.

CHAPTER NINE

SOME UNIVERSITY PEOPLE

The Trustees

Certain trustees have been known to interfere with the educational aims and processes of the university whose affairs they are supposed to be looking after. But these interfering trustees have almost always ended by getting a large amount of unfavorable publicity, making themselves look ridiculous, bringing unrest and shame to their university, and, in the long run, accomplishing nothing. A businessman trustee has about as much business trying to solve specific educational problems as a professor of Sanskrit would have trying to run a bank. The successful specialist in one field is more than likely to behave like an ass in another field.

By and large, however, it must be said that trustees have understood their limitations as professional educators, and have commendably steered far from the seething waters of strictly educational methods and aims. Only a few of them have made asses of themselves; most of them have shown a rather extraordinary self-restraint in the presence of matters that must sometimes have vexed them, grieved them, or confused them. The absurdities

194

of the few who have acted like the trustee in Thurber's *The Male Animal* have brought contempt and suspicion on the many. This is unfortunate. Most trustees of American universities have done a first-class job of attending strictly and efficiently to their business of administering the financial affairs of the university, and selecting its top-ranking officers. They deserve more credit than the public (remembering the few absurd trustees) is inclined to give them.

The President

The number of university presidents who have made asses of themselves is considerably greater (as records of the American Association of University Professors indicate) than that of trustees similarly unfortunate. The reason why presidents make asses of themselves sometimes often is that most of them have been professors before they were presidents.

On the other hand, the percentage of able and efficient presidents is probably much higher than that of able and efficient professors. Besides, it is much easier to run an organization smoothly than to teach human beings properly.

The chief source of weakness among presidents is their tenure of office. A president is usually appointed for life. Ambitious and conscientious, he is normally a wonder-man for a few years. After that, as he grows older and sees his initial reforms well established in the universty, he becomes a "strong" administrator well versed in the art of making the university run efficiently, though not necessarily in a forward direction. He may preside over a smooth-running stationary engine. Gradually, as the years pass and he sees how well he is conducting the university, he must struggle hard to keep from acquiring a God-complex in which he mistakes himself for the Creator. When he begins to lose this struggle, his tenure should end, and he should be retired on a distinguished professorship with a well-earned pension.

His retirement will allow new ideas to enter the university; it will break up the palace guard of favorites and yes-men he has gathered about himself during the years; and it will bring in another wonder-man who will carry the university on through another spurt of progress. A university whose fixed policy is to cling to a president till he reaches the age of seventy inevitably begins to slow down, and eventually to stagnate; and the president himself becomes a pompous cipher.

The Administrative Professor

A good many professors are called on to be deans, sub-deans, registrars, provosts, bursars, heads of committees and colleges, and so on. This is tempting work. It enables the professor to bolster up his deep-lying sense of inferiority by becoming a large fish in a small pond. The older and wiser professors (perhaps after some youthful experience of splashing about in the pond) do not often yield to the temptation of these jobs, but instead, strictly cultivate their own gardens. The dangers in yielding are too many.

One danger is that they lose delight in learning, and care more for the head-turning busy-ness of committees, conferences, administrative planning, meeting V.I.P.'s at luncheons, speaking to organizations, and so on, than they care about either learning or teaching. It is simply impossible for a man to be a good professor and a good executive simultaneously for any length of time. Being a good professor is a full-time job all by itself.

Sometimes, of course, the good professor may carry over into an executive position a head of steam sufficient to make him both a good professor and a good executive for a few years. But the head of steam inevitably dissipates, and the executive-professor becomes merely an executive. That is why no professor who continues to teach should be continued in any executive position more than two or three years.

But the greatest danger in a professor's becoming an executive is that, practically always, he loses his humanity. This is bad for him as a man and as a professor, and it is bad for the students (for whom, after all, the university exists). He begins to see the university, or his part of it, as a team, a system, a machine. He forgets that a university cannot possibly afford to be an organization, that it must always be a *collection of individual human beings*. The entire business of a university is not to develop human cogs and cotter pins valuable only in relation to a larger mechanism, but to develop independent human personalities intrinsically valuable. But the administrator, eager to make a success of his job, convinced that it is vitally important that the university machine run smoothly, asks, or rather, demands, insists, with much figurative if not actual fist-pounding, that every individual within the university do his part as a cog or a cotter pin in making the engine run without a sputter. The rules must not be broken, and there must be no exceptions. The welfare of the organization permits no allowances for human nature, for experiments, for mistakes, for the excesses and follies of youth; the rules do not recognize the individual and the irregular; the system makes no official provision for human sympathy, human understanding, human pity, human love, human forgiveness. If any university student happens to have originality or individuality, dislike of arbitrary authority, desire to ask questions, uncustomary creativeness, ideas of his own about what is good for him, resentment at playing the part of a cog or a cotter pin — he had better walk softly, stay clear of the administration, and hide his true nature under a bushel. If he doesn't, some of the professor-administrators are going to give him trouble.

It must be added that, by and large, the professor-administrators from the humanities departments do not offend in this respect so much as do the scientists-turned-administrators. The latter expect and demand that students conduct their lives with the precision of fine machines and the inevitability of a formula. This is a sad thing. It is sad for a professor, considered merely as a human being, to lose sight of humanity in tending the wheels of an organization; it is sad for the professor, considered merely as a mind, not to be able to perceive the stultifying effect of conformity; it is sad for the student to have his mind forced into uniform and his personality looked upon as a cog or a cotter pin; it is sad for the university not to recognize that flesh-and-blood human beings are more worth cherishing than is the abstraction of any organization; it is sad for society to have to depend on only those graduates who have learned to conform.

It is a perversion of the very purpose of the university, a bed of Procrustes, where the individual is warped to make him fit the organization. This does not mean, of course, that any one individual shall be allowed to disturb the lives of other individuals: simple consideration of other people is essential. But these are not the matters with which the professor-administrator is usually concerned. His problems involve matters like grade requirements, credit requirements, attendance requirements, promptness requirements, form-filling requirements, excuses, parking fines, chapel attendance, and like offenses, not offenses against people, but against the rules of the organization .

Here are some examples of what I mean. Last year a student lacked one full credit for graduation; he returned to the university to make up the credit, but since no student could register for less than three courses, he took three courses and passed them all. Then, a week before he was to get his diploma, it was discovered that he lacked half a credit in some "required" subject; someone in the registrar's office had made a mistake in signing him up for the three courses. He was officially ineligible for graduation, and he got no degree.

Then there was the student who could make A's and B's in all courses but a mathematics course that was "required." He seemed to be completely lacking in mathematical perception. The only thing that could be done for him was to make him a Physical Education major (along with the football players), where he would be excused from mathematics, but would also be compelled to take a large number of Physical Education courses that he did not want, and for which he had only contempt.

And there was the girl who fell in love when she was a freshman, and failed out of the university. Five years later, at great sacrifice, she returned to the university, and was admitted on condition that she make no grade lower than a C. As it turned out, she made three A's, a

B, and a D — the last being given by a young instructor who had never taught before, and missing a C by only two points. The girl was dropped again, with the result that it will be virtually impossible for her, with a record of being dropped twice already from a university, to gain admittance to any other first-class university.

Instances like these could be catalogued by the hour. It is in dealing with such problems that the professor-administrator loses his sense of the essential purpose of a university, his humanity, and his value as an educator. This happens almost invariably, I am sorry to say, and especially if he is a scientist.

If I were a university president, I should insist that every one of my faculty administrators should keep always prominently displayed in his office a very large sign with the words: "The letter killeth, but the spirit giveth life."

The Research Professor

"Research," says Bertrand Russell, "is at least as important as education, when we are considering the functions of universities in the life of mankind."

The modern university has replaced the medieval monastery as the home of the scholar and the scientist; and the modern professor is, in many ways, the equivalent of the medieval monk, cloistered from the world but busy with matters that involve the world's progress. Nevertheless, there are indications that research in the universities may not be so important "in the life of mankind" as it was when Russell wrote in 1926. Industry is supporting more and more research, even in fields not immediately utilitarian. And governments all over the world cannot fill their demands for researchers. It is possible that eventually university professors will constitute a very minor portion of the world's professional researchers.

Notwithstanding this possibility, the university cannot afford to lose the reseach professor. No one who is not a researcher can teach students to be researchers; and no professor can convey to his students a sense of delight in learning unless he himself has that delight. Nothing could be less inspiring to a student than a professor who has learned nothing since he passed his Ph.D. examinations, and cares to learn nothing else.

Furthermore, a professor who delights in learning should delight in letting other people share in what he has currently learned, through publication, through "papers" read to colleagues at professional conventions, through lectures to the public and to specialized groups at his own university, and through lectures and talks to classes. Delight in learning should not be hidden under a bushel.

On the other hand, the pressure for publication in the great universities is shameless and demoralizing. It results in so few benefits and so many really vicious evils that one can only be amazed that universities even tolerate it, much less encourage it. I am speaking here not of regular and steady research, with publication at irregular (and sometimes lengthy) intervals, but of insistence on publication at a mad and unremitting pace.

The benefit chiefly prized by this frenzied search after publication is the reputation a university acquires by having on its faculty many professors whose names appear in many journals many times a year. All the other virtues a university may possess (unless it be a championship football team) count as nothing compared to this one advertising gimmick.

"The advancement of knowledge for the good of mankind" is the second (and, of course, the official and highly respectable) reason that the universities give for demanding constant publication by their faculties. Unfortunately, however, it is not regard for "the good of mankind" that inspires the typical research professor, or that makes the university spur him on to perpetual publication. It is promotion for the professor, and publicity for the university. In most major universities, promotion (where it does not go to the president's old friends) goes to the professor who publishes most. It makes little difference *what* he publishes, since almost nobody reads it, anyhow; and nobody but a few specialists widely scattered over the world can judge whether or not it is sound. As for the amount of "good" done to mankind, it is nil in 99.9 per cent of the publications. All that matters is that the professor publish *something*, and publish *often*.

This general policy of universities has so much against it that one cannot but be astonished that it is retained. In the first place, "it would be the greatest mistake," as Whitehead says, "to estimate the value of each member of a faculty by the printed work signed with his name." He goes on to explain that "For some of the most fertile minds composition in writing . . . seems to be an impossibility. In every faculty you will find that some of the more brilliant teachers are not among those who publish." The fact is that anybody and everybody with a month's training in methods and source materials, with elementary knowledge of almost any subject, and with normal mentality, can do publishable research. Indeed, when one looks into the oceans of articles appearing in the learned journals, one is convinced that anybody and everybody *is* publishing.

In the next place, pressure for publication results in the undermining of professorial moral standards. Knowing that promotion depends upon publication, researchers continually distort, suppress, and deliberately falsify their data in order to achieve publication. This essential dishonesty is more common among scientists than among scholars, for scientists, working privately in field or laboratory, can say they got whatever results they were looking for — and nobody can prove them wrong. Other scientists can go over the same ground, and then write courteously in a journal, "Our experiments and observations do not confirm the results obtained by Professor X." Whereupon Professor X., smelling in the wind another item for his annual bibliography, writes an article criticizing the experiments and observations of his critics; whereupon *they* write articles defending themselves, and getting more items for *their* bibliography . . . and on and on. Actually, however, even this sort of interchange is not likely to happen; most researchers are too busy with their own specific problems to bother about repeating studies by previous workers.

Deliberate dishonesty is probably not very common among research professors; honest research is so easy that they have no need of being dishonest. Nevertheless, I could give detailed particulars about flagrant, deliberate, and inexcusable dishonesty that I myself know about among at least six much-respected American scientists; and it is impossible, by the very nature of the subject, that I could have personal knowledge of more than a fraction of one percent of the dishonesties that have happened all about me during my university career. On the other hand, half-conscious dishonesty (including misquotation, quotation out of context, disregard for all unfavorable data, self-persuasion that borderline data are really positive, obsession with one point of view so that evidence for other points of view becomes psychologically imperceptible, and so on) is obvious in nearly every published paper. These dishonesties are due, of course, to the universal pressure for publication; without this pressure, the professors would not be tempted.

But the saddest thing about the frenzied research-for-publication is the havoc it wreaks with the professor as teacher. The tangible rewards, in promotion and salary, resulting from publication (no matter how trivial) are so obvious that the professor, in justice to himself and to his family, cannot really afford to spend much time as a teacher. His lectures can consist of readings from textbooks written by somebody else; his papers can be graded by student graders, or not at all; the time he gives to all his students individually may be one hour a week, or no time at all. But nobody cares so long as he publishes his little articles at regular intervals. Just as I began this section, I received a letter from a former student now finishing his graduate work in another university, and preparing for a new job as teacher in still another university. He writes: "My main test will be this next year when I am teaching full-time. It is then that I will have to see whether I can keep up with my own work in spite of the continual pressure of classes, seeing students, and great stacks of papers each week. Dr. B. [director of his graduate work] says you have to be ruthless, and just whip off the grading, and let the students fend for themselves, because you've got your own work to do, and would go under yourself if you let them take up as much time as ideally you would perhaps want to give them."

Dr. B. is right. No ambitious professor can afford to spend much time on his students. Let them fend for themselves. In all my years about the university, I have known one man who was denied tenure because of poor teaching; but I have known dozens who were denied tenure because they did not publish regularly. I well remember one particularly flagrant case in which a new instructor in a great university happened to be ideally suited, by temperament and background, for teaching English to the sensitive, proud, and emotional Latin Americans who attended the university by the hundreds. He made such a phenomenal success, with praise from students and faculty alike, that the administrative officers in charge of the work raised his rank and salary, and gave him tenure. At once, a more typical professor from a quite different field discovered that the instructor had never done any published research, and protested so loudly that the administration had to back down, rescind its promotion, and by implication drive the instructor from the university.

Good teaching counts for nothing at all in the major universities. To be sure, presidents and heads of departments are continually protesting that, oh, yes, good teaching is, too, recognized and rewarded. But this is 99 per cent fiction.

As a part of his negativistic attitude toward teaching, the regular research-publisher develops character traits and attitudes of mind that are as tragic for him as for his students. Exalting publication above everything else, he loses his human touch, develops a eunuchoid callousness to the feelings of others, approaches the hard impersonality of the Prussian. He resents student intrusion on him; he grows ironic over the problems that are troubling them; in his solitary study or laboratory, insulated from growing life, he becomes incapable of comprehending the pains of other human beings; and, by seeing his name in print so often, and receiving promotion so regularly, he is more than likely to develop delusions of grandeur that (when combined with the pressure under which he works to produce his articles and books) make him irritable when students question him, arrogant when they ask for help, indifferent if they learn nothing or desire to learn nothing. The scientist who is trying to "advance knowledge for the good of mankind," is not usually much interested in the good of mankind when it comes to his office door in the form of a student; and the scholar who is devoting his life to "humane letters" is seldom notably humane toward young people who need help.

I repeat that what I have said here is *not* a condemnation of research and publication. I repeat that research and publication are absolutely essential for every professor, essential for his own soul and for the souls of those he teaches. But I must say that I have something less than respect for that common policy of universities and administrations which puts excessive pressure on faculties for constant publication; the publication of trivia, of trash, of superficial reports, of dishonest articles. What is needed is less publication, better publication, and recognition that a professor's chief moral responsibility is toward his students, not toward the task of getting his name in print.

The Alumni

University alumni have been so often, so universally, and so justly ridiculed that one is tempted to search deliberately for something nice to say about them. But it is difficult to find anything. Of course, in order to find something nice to say about the alumni, one must distinguish between the alumnus as an individual and the alumnus as a member of some organized alumni activity. The former is generally much nicer than the latter, and is not included in subsequent remarks about alumni.

No doubt alumni organizations have an important influence in helping shape the attitude of many graduates toward their Alma Mater. Thus, alumni organizations may help create a reservoir of good will in a community, and this good will may make life and education more pleasant for both students and professors at the university. Students and professors in a community where they are generally hated cannot operate successfully. In addition, alumni who have been influenced by the organization, as well as nonalumni in the community, may be helpful in finding jobs for young graduates, or in granting scholarships, donating to the library, and leaving legacies to the university. Sometimes, indeed, the alumni organization itself may raise money directly for the benefit of the university, though, as a rule, the amount of money they raise is comparatively minuscule. For these benefits, or possible benefits, the universities are willing to put up with one Homecoming Day per year. The price is a bit high, to be sure; but, in the long run, the bargain is probably a good one.

Presumably the alumni themselves enjoy Homecoming Day. It gives the good businessmen among them a chance to advertise themselves; it gives the politicians who have been unable or unwilling to enter real politics a chance to exercise their talents in a modest way; it gives the "unsuccessful" ones a chance to make some worthwhile contacts; it gives the "successful" ones a chance to lord it a bit over those who disregarded them in undergraduate days; it gives most of them a chance to prove to the world and to themselves that they have actually been to college, a fact not otherwise easily discernible.

But perhaps the alumni enjoy Homecoming Day most of all because it helps them recapture something of their youth and its imagined joys. The joys they hope to re-capture are, from an educational point of view, most instructive. They are the joys of a football game, of seeing the old campus where they spent four youthful years, of social intercourse, of meeting old friends and old lovers, and perhaps of meeting a professor who (for a wonder) broke a rule and was kind to them twenty years before. *But they do not try to recapture the joys of the classroom and of learning.*

Why this hiatus? Could it be that they never had any joy in the classroom and in learning? And if so, whose fault was it? I have heard that, very rarely, some alumnus on Homecoming Day spends an hour in a classroom listening to the lecture of a former professor. But no pro-fessor has ever told me personally that it happened to him. This is another bit of evidence concerning the edu-cational failure of the universities.

The Students

Undoubtedly many high schools in America are not properly preparing their students for college. The stu-dents should learn more foreign languages than they do, simply because young people can generally catch on to a foreign language more easily than older people. If they plan to enter scientific fields, they should learn more mathematics than many of them do. Above all, they should have more thorough training in writing and reading English. Early training in chemistry and physics does not seem to be essential. Very few Americans had chemistry and physics in high school; and even if they had those subjects, they had only a year of each, at a very elementary level. Yet American chemists and physicists have been doing very well in the world. In certain specialized branches of chemistry and physics, the scientists of other nations may be ahead of our own; but I think it is generally conceded that, by and large, American chemists and physicists are as good as any others anywhere. We just don't have enough of them; and the colleges are to blame.

The trouble with our high school graduates is not so much that they are ill-prepared, as that they are, at best, likely to be indifferent to learning, and, at worst, more than likely to regard learning as an intolerable labor, teachers as vengeful taskmasters, classrooms as minor prisons, books as offensive bores, and the entire educational process as tyrannical and unpleasant. Only a small percentage manage to move outside this drab system, and revolve in a circle where learning seems to them exciting and joyous. All this is most disturbing, especially in view of the fact that nearly all students in elementary school, and even in junior high, take delight in the process of learning and intellectual exploration. Somewhere along the line, however, that "first fine careless rapture" is lost; and the high school graduates reach the university as already damaged goods. If they learn at all, it is only because they are driven by a sense of duty to something that they vaguely comprehend, by parental adjurations, by habit, by desire for the financial security said to lie at the end of four years in college, and by eagerness to conform to the conduct that their social class expects of them. Hardly one in ten learns for the love of learning.

I do not know why the change from the eager elementary pupil to the bored high school senior occurs. But I think it is a result of the exposure of the child's growing intelligence to the unrealities and artificialities of high school education. On the one hand, the child sees movies and television, listens to the radio, reads newspapers and magazines, begins to move about in the world outside his home. Very quickly he begins to recognize advertising, promotion, and propaganda for what they are. He notices that each of five different beers and ten different cigarettes proclaims daily that it is the best in the world, and he can hardly help drawing the conclusion that somebody is paying millions of dollars to help cultivate a lie. He is told that he should respect his government and the duly elected officials of his city, state, and nation; but he is daily exposed to headlines revealing corruption in high places, to editorials condemning the folly or the corruption of high officials, to political speakers and news commentators discussing the folly or the corruption of government. He is told that private business conducted on a high ethical plane is the basis of this country's greatness; but he has seen his family stung again and again by some dishonesty in business, knows that when he himself goes shopping he must keep a watchful eye to avoid being cheated, and (if he has a summer job) notes from the inside some of the sharp practices of employers. He is told that he should respect the law; but whenever he runs afoul of it, even in a mere speeding or parking ticket, he finds that the "cops" are likely to be ignorant and arrogant brutes, the judges authoritarian and too busy to be just, the police system cruel and unintelligent. He is told by his parents and his preacher and his teachers that he should devote himself humbly and unselfishly to being a good citizen, looking out for the welfare of others; but he sees everywhere, even in his own parents, pride of possession, material ambition, selfish striving, and obvious hypocrisy. If he has a grain of intelligence he must sense the discrepancies between what he has been told and what he has discovered for himself about the world.

This sharp-minded, worldly wise, disillusioned young person is sent into a high school dedicated to inculcating unrealistic "truths" and upholding intellectual positions at variance with everything that he himself has observed in the world. What else, under the circumstances, can be expected of him except that he be bored, indifferent, hostile, averse to learning the fictions he is daily taught? "The idea that falsehood is edifying," says Bertrand Russell, "is one of the besetting sins of those who draw up educational schemes." Clever young people are taught these falsehoods, and then "when they grow up and discover the truth, the result is too often a complete cynicism." If the high schools were allowed (by parents, government, church, and community) to teach the plain facts, well known to every researcher in the field, about sex, religion, morality, history, politics, government, business, and law, the students would be avid for knowledge. Nothing could stop them from learning. Meanwhile, the wonder is that any students at all retain the slighest willingness to learn in those houses of equivocation that are called high schools.

Yet (miracle of miracles!) a scant handful of them do manage to run the gauntlet of high school without losing their early enthusiasm for learning. It is a tribute to the undying optimism and persistent curiosity of the human animal. This scant handful of students consists of two types of minds: cheerful young cynics who see through the fog, and do not let it trouble them; and simple, unworldly, protected youths who have not matured, who do not notice any discrepancies between high school ideals and the realities of life, and who still believe in the stork.

In any event, the material that the high schools hand over to the universities is not (except for the scant handful just mentioned) ideal; it has been botched in the making. On the other hand, it is not completely ruined; with a little care in the universities, much of it can be saved. The material is still fresh, still ductile, still sufficiently excited by the new environment to be eagerly co-operative. It is not too late for the universities to shape something worth while out of this material. But the universities fail with most of it.

A more detailed description of this material may belong here. It may be conveniently divided into four groups:

One group consists of those cheerful young cynics mentioned above. They manage to shrug off the absurdities and the deficiencies of the university as they did those of the high school; and they usually do well at the university.

The second group consists of those young innocents who have not become aware of the discrepancies between life-as-it-is and life-as-it-is-taught. These, when brought face to face with the slightly more heterodox, or at least slightly odd, views of most university professors, may react in either of two ways. They may be quite unable to assimilate the new views, in which case they quietly pack their belongings and go home; or they may prove to have sturdy digestive systems that can take care of the new views, in which case they become some of the best students in the university.

The third group are those who regard instructors as taskmasters, learning as drudgery, and the educational system a tyrant against which every self-respecting student should rebel by means of rule-breaking and hell-raising at every opportunity. Occasionally, by their third or fourth year, some of these students may awake to the fact that the university is an opportunity, not a disagreeable necessity. On the other hand, the university itself, by its own behavior, probably impels as many students (from the group just above and the one just below) into this category as it retrieves from it. Most of the group get through the university somehow, do not let it affect them except in their habits of drinking and social intercourse, and forget about it ever afterward.

But by far the greatest number of freshmen who have undergone the selective processes of high school and university admissions requirements are merely nice, subdued young boys and girls who have learned to do exactly what they have been told to do in high school, have never consciously or openly questioned the unrealistic disciplines of high school, have never had any original thoughts (never having been shown that there are any original thoughts to be had), have never given anybody any trouble, have been able to accommodate within themselves (without apparent indigestion) the lion of the world and the lamb of the school room. They have been able to make this accommodation because they have been caught up in habit, in a routine of dutiful obedience; and protected by it, they do not need to think. Most of those who are accepted into a university will do their best to learn what they are told to learn. But they will not learn it well or enthusiastically because they have never been shown that learning can be delightful. Their learning will affect only the most superficial layers of their personality, and will remain with them only so long as the final examination lasts. This kind of student is the major stock-in-trade of every university.

It may be significant that, in the local high school I have already mentioned in this book (the one which is considered by a national committee to be one of the best 38 in the United States, and one of the two best in the state) the most recent list of honor students (358 names) consists of *70 per cent girls!* I am certainly no antifeminist, but I cannot believe that girls are that much brighter than boys. It seems perfectly obvious that all those girls got on the honor list because they were nice, sweet, obedient, conventional, conformist, unoriginal, neat young things who tried to please their teachers, do as they were told, and never give anybody any trouble by questioning, objecting, doubting, or thinking outside the accepted channels.

Perhaps many in this fourth group are irretrievably damaged before they reach the university. Their habit of obedience may be too deeply ingrained to be easily eradicated. On the other hand, since they are still young, plastic, and cooperative, many of them could undoubtedly be saved. But precious few *are* saved. They encounter in the university too many stupid professors, smug professors, arrogant professors, indifferent professors, personally maladjusted professors, impersonal professors-turned-executive, unfriendly and uncharitable professors, and professors who think it is their duty to "weed out absolutely mercilessly" those who do not conform to the university's codes. Salvation is still remote for most of our university students.

CHAPTER TEN

SCHIZOPHRENIA AMONG THE DEPARTMENTS

In this chapter I am discussing only the college of arts and sciences in the university; what is said does not apply to the professional schools (engineering, architecture, medicine, etc.). The argument between these two groups — between those who value Education for the Sake of Education and those who value Education for the Sake of a Livelihood is old; and I doubt if anything new could be contributed here.

Practically all the professors in the College of Arts and Sciences teach their courses with the customary professorial symptoms of mild schizophrenia. They can seldom make up their minds whether they are teaching their courses for the benefit of future specialists (students who are planning to do postgraduate work in chemistry, biology, military history, economics, literary history, and so on), or whether they are teaching for the benefit of students who need to know the basic principles and facts of a subject, for the sake of being educated, but have no intention of specializing in the field. Apparently there is a longing among the professors to produce highly trained specialists, but at the same time a vague realization that,

216

if the truth were faced, very few of the students in any course are planning to be highly trained specialists in that field. Hardly one professor in ten can make up his mind about this problem; and therefore nine out of ten teach bastardized courses that are neither flesh nor fish. And nine out of ten students are forced to spend a great amount of their time learning detailed information that can have no bearing on what the students intend to do later in life, no bearing on their fundamental thought patterns, and no bearing on the process by which they become genuinely educated men and women. The amount of time and good intellectual effort wasted thus is almost criminal.

The Science Departments

In general, the best research and the worst teaching in the university are done in the science departments. Reasons for the bad teaching are many:

First, in this preponderantly scientific age, when the rewards of scientific research are so rich, the science professor is almost irresistibly tempted to spend as little time as possible in the comparatively unrewarding job of teaching. He just does not bother to try to be a good teacher.

Second, none of the sciences (except psychology and anthropology) deals with human beings as human beings. The typical science professor is not equipped by training or by experience to understand people, and has no particular interest in trying to understand them or perceive their needs.

Third, steeped as he is in the rigorous disciplines of exactness, impartiality, and the effort to eliminate the personal equation, the typical science professor actually tries hard to maintain an impersonal, impartial attitude toward his students, not to let his sympathies stand in the way of his "duty." He wants to be strictly "just" in dealing with students, which means conforming to all rules and regulations that he himself has established, and considers sacred and inviolable. He is likely to feel guilty whenever any human emotion betrays him into looking upon his students as anything more then identical units in an impersonal (and rather boring) experiment.

Fourth, the science professor's whole life is devoted to trying to find general laws to express the peculiarities of particular phenomena. Almost instinctively, he resents the unique and the unclassifiable, the unorthodox and the individual, the nonconforming and the unaccountable. Yet, if a human being is worth anything at all, he is worth it not as a fixed unit in a system, but as an independent, autonomous, free-wheeling personality. Any educational theory or method that would have him otherwise is dangerous to the individual student, and also to democratic society. The science professor, therefore, is caught in a schizophrenic dilemma: every instinct within him urges him to treat students as uniform natural phenomena, and to construct some formalized method by which all students may be educated alike; yet if he treats them that way, he is violating the democratic theory which has put the student in the university in the first place.

Finally, the science professor is accustomed to seeing natural phenomena behave in uniform and predictable ways: hydrogen always acts like hydrogen, malaria is always transmitted by mosquitoes, the sum of the squares on the two sides of a right triangle is equal to the square on the hypotenuse. But human beings don't always behave in uniform and predictable ways. It is disconcerting and irritating to the scientist. He expects his students to behave in uniform and predictable ways; and when they don't, he frets, scolds, disciplines, punishes, worries. He simply cannot bring himself to accept the humanity of human beings.

Because mathematics is the fundamental science, exemplifying the major educational weaknesses of science in their purest form, the *Mathematics Department* usually has the worst teachers in the university. Moreover, there does seem to be, in some people, a certain inborn mathematical facility, or talent, like the talent for music, which makes mathematics come easily for them. These specially endowed persons, when they are teachers, are unable to perceive why others cannot understand the seemingly obvious. Therefore they become impatient and unsympathetic teachers who attribute the failure of their students to "lack of sufficient work" or "obstinate stupidity." At the same time, their own gift of mathematical intuition, when compared to the plugging and obfuscated struggles of other people, gives the mathematician a sense of his own superiority, a characteristic arrogance. It need hardly be added that this special gift (like the gift of music, poetry, or painting) does not prevent a mathematician from sometimes being a great fool, nor does it prevent him from being a wise man. But as a teacher he is usually unworldly, conceited, unable to understand or to teach any but the most naturally gifted students.

As might be expected, the teachers in the *Physics Department* are often not much better than the mathematicians. The atmosphere of physics is almost as rarefied as that of mathematics. In addition, now that developments in nuclear physics have become so wildly spectacular, the excitement of research in physics almost obliterates any interest the physicist may have in being a teacher. Furthermore, modern physics has become so largely a matter of "teamwork" that the solitary worker, the lone wolf, the individualistic mind, the student who prefers independence to collaboration, finds here a cold welcome. On the other hand, the physics professor is seldom so intellectually arrogant as the typical mathematics professor; he is more humble in the face of the immense amount of knowledge that he knows he doesn't have.

The *Chemistry Department* usually has excellent professors for a certain type of student, the one who has a good memory, is a steady plodder, lacks intellectual daring, and has little true originality of mind. Since the majority of students are of this type, the majority of chemistry professors satisfy the students quite well, and teach them something. The fact that, on the whole, chemistry professors are less criticized than almost any others, is not because they are good teachers; it is because they have mediocre students.

The *Biology Department* is in a strange stage of development just now. The theory of evolution, which gave point to all biological activities up to the 1920's, has been well established, and worked almost to death. As a result, biological science in an outward direction (that is, research in the larger world of nature) has become hardly more than a descriptive science concerning new species and subspecies, their life histories and habits. But in the other direction, inward biology (that is, research in physiology, genetics, biochemistry, medical work, and biological experiments with fissionable materials) is as exciting as physics. The typical professor in the first type of biology mentioned is likely to be either a warm-hearted eccentric or an ingenuous victim of an inferiority complex. The typical professor of the second type of biology cares as little for his students as does the physics professor or the mathematics professor, and is generally quite as bad a teacher.

The professors of the *Psychology Department* ought, in theory, to be the best in the university. As a matter of fact, they are usually quite bad. Perhaps the reason is that many psychology professors entered their field because they were not far from being psychological cases themselves. They have odd obsessions that prevent them from seeing how badly they bore their students; and they know so much about human nature that they are always balancing between the horns of a schizophrenic dilemma: not venturing to make a choice for better or for worse, and not presuming to lead the student anywhere, or teach him much. Nevertheless, the psychology professor nearly always *means* well. He has the right attitude toward teaching; that is, he regards his students as individually unique human beings with human feelings, weaknesses, peculiarities; he is not afraid of originality in a student; he objects to standardizing and uniformizing students; he would like to see the student develop as an independent personality. The only trouble with him is that his hands are tied by his own eccentricities, obsessions, and timidities.

The Liberal Arts Departments

Most of the liberal arts departments suffer likewise from chronic schizophrenia. The professors cannot make up their minds whether they want to be scholars or interpreters, whether they want to be delvers after facts, or original thinkers, whether they want to teach what is known and recorded, or voice personal criticism and appreciation. Shall the English professor explain just what Shakespeare said, or shall he go farther and try to evaluate the dramatic effectiveness of this scene or that and the psychological subtleties of the characters? Shall the history professor tell the bare facts of the Roosevelt administrations, or shall he tell, in addition, his own pet theories about the economic, cultural, philosophical, and psychological forces that produced the facts? Shall the philosophy professor be satisfied with explaining what Kant thought, or shall he go beyond explanation to criticism and evaluation in the light of his own private philosophy?

All such questions are further complicated by the fact that Shakespeare, Roosevelt, and Kant have been the subject of numerous prior evaluations, appreciations, criticisms, and explanations; and the liberal arts professor has to decide how many of these he himself is going to evaluate, appreciate, criticize, and explain. Here are wheels within wheels.

As a rule, the liberal arts professor tends toward the factual, the unoriginal approach. He does this for several reasons. One is that he feels incompetent to use any other approach. Another is that he wants to emulate the scientists by being impersonal and impartial. Furthermore (again under the influence of the scientists) he is inclined to regard the world's literature, history, and philosophy as a vast storehouse (like nature for the scientist) which he must explore for the sake of "increasing knowledge." And finally, he knows that it is usually profitable to steer clear of the controversial: promotion comes much more quickly to the professor who merely adds another dry dust particle to the heap accumulating in the learned journals.

At any rate, if the ambitious professor does wish to say anything new, it had better be about something that nobody cares much about, something safe in the mummified past. The quickest way for a liberal arts professor to condemn himself to campus obscurity is to take for his field anything that has been written in the last fifty years, and express ideas about it. (It must be said that this attitude is showing signs of weakening, but not in the greater universities.) This unwillingness to deal with the still-vital, together with the desire to approach the well-dead in the strictly impartial manner of the scientist, is one reason why the liberal arts students generally receive their instruction with something less than enthusiasm. When they register in courses in order to find out about great poets, novelists, playwrights, and philosophers, they expect cake, but too often receive instead a dry crust of pedantry.

The *English Department* is, perhaps, the most complexly schizophrenic of all the liberal arts departments. In the first place, its professors, who are English professors chiefly because they are interested in literature, are saddled with the unsought burden of teaching freshmen how to spell, punctuate, make grammatical sentences, and construct logical themes. Nobody with the slightest imagination could want this job. For this reason, the older professors shuffle off the major part of the job upon young instructors and graduate students — most of whom never had a real course in writing (and often not even in grammar) in their lives, and have not the slightest ability to teach or criticize writing. Which is one reason why we hear so much about the deficiencies of students in the writing of English.

But this is not the only divided aspect of the English Department. Robert Graves, in *The Crowning Privilege*, tells of a young woman studying literature at Cambridge: "I asked her, what poems do you enjoy most? and she answered with dignity: poems are not meant to be enjoyed, they are meant to be analyzed." (By the way, what a picnic the young English instructor would have with the punctuation of *that* sentence!) The typical English professor has trained himself to care little about imparting any joy he may feel in literature, and not to wonder whether his students enjoy literature.

He will maintain, of course, that full enjoyment is not possible unless we know the date of some old drama, say, its source, the way in which it differs from its source, its first presentation, the conditions of its discovery, the place this particular drama has in the author's career, the way in which the drama reflects the temper of the age in which it was written, the influence it has had on subsequent drama, and the history of its production on the stage. For the sake of the argument, let us admit (a large admission!) that the professor is right in saying that the student cannot enjoy the drama without all these scholastic trappings. But the great difficulty is simply: here the professor halts. When he is just getting ready to help the student enjoy the drama, he drops the subject. The student, therefore, following the instructor's lead, has no reason to think there is anything to the drama but its scholastic trappings. Nine times out of ten he listens to the professor, learns what the professor says, passes the examinations, gets a credit in the course — and never once sees the drama as a work of art intended to give aesthetic pleasure, never thinks of it again, or reads it, or lets it enter into the molding of his personality, or permits it to affect his world-view, his life-view, or his God-view. All the imagination of the dramatist, the emotion, the intellect, the shaping creativity, the aesthetic will that has forced inchoate life into a pattern of beauty, the meaning of the pattern itself — all this the student misses. English classes are filled with the dead hopes of young people who had thought that they might be given a view into the hearts of the world's great writers, but got instead only the superficial trappings of scholasticism.

The same kind of schizophrenia affects the *Language Departments.* Here the professors whose chief interest is literature are compelled to teach grammar at the kindergarten level. Often the language departments solve this problem by having young instructors and graduate students teach the elementary courses. Contrary to the situation in the English Department, this solution is probably as good as can be had. The young teacher has always had four or five years of study in the language, he has the enthusiasm of one who is still learning, he does not know the language so well that it has ceased to be a challenge to him. Most of the time, unless he is conceited, he makes an excellent teacher. On the other hand, though the teacher may be good, the methods of teaching modern languages in the university are descended directly from the old methods of teaching Latin — a dead language. French, German, Spanish, Italian, Portuguese, and Russian are usually taught for reading purposes and philological background only. If it be granted that modern languages should be taught as if they were dead languages, then the the language departments probably do a better job of teaching than any other department in the liberal arts college. There are two exceptions to this generalization: one is the elementary class presided over by a bored older teacher; the other is the German Department, where a stern North German spirit of Lutheranism and Prussianism is likely to prevail, so that the students find learning a joyless duty and a deadly serious chore.

Courses in the *History Department* are, as a rule, the university's most perfect type of the fact-loaded, idea-absent, academic exercise. Here the wood is everywhere lost among the trees; and it is the rare professor who can show the student anything but a close-clustered thicket of details. While the professor lectures on the Battle of Cowpens, the strategy of the Battle of Cowpens, the tactics of the Battle of Cowpens, the logistics of the Battle of Cowpens, the personalities of the opposing generals in the Battle of Cowpens, the classroom swims around, and the great ideas and forces of history are lost in the flood of facts. Certainly, facts are interesting in themselves, facts about the Battle of Cowpens should be preserved, and specialists in military history should know all about this battle. But need a student spend his time learning all the known facts about it? Cannot history be taught so as to have a meaningful relationship to law, literature, philosophy, religion, art, architecture; and a meaningful relationship to the fundamental motives, habits, aspirations, psychological peculiarities, self-deceptions, hypocrisies, and grandeurs of human nature; and a meaningful relationship to the present? Must history be taught only as a potpourri of details to be memorized for a test, and forgotten immediately afterward? Apparently the professors of history think so. And since a majority of the students have never learned that anything is more important than memorizing, the majority of students are satisfied with the majority of history professors.

The *Philosophy Department* is almost the saddest in the university; its case of schizophrenia is the worst. Yet the case is very simple. The Philosophy Department is dedicated to the study and the revelation of elemental truths; yet, by the nature of its place in the university and in the community, it is virtually forbidden to explore large areas of thought that would do violence to current religious beliefs and moral practices. If the Philosophy Department were not fundamentally optimistic, idealistic, Christian, and conventionally moral in its doctrines, the parents of the students taking philosophy courses would make such an outcry that the department would be shattered. Whether materialism, mechanism, pessimism, paganism, amorality, and atheism are logically and scientifically "sound" is not the most important question; what matters is that the students in philosophy courses hardly even hear about them, and are certainly never made fully acqainted with them and their arguments. The existence of these "evils" must never be revealed to students by a Philosophy Department that, by its very name, is committed to the revelation of knowledge.

Almost as bad as this hush-hush attitude toward certain views of truth is the refusal of the Philosophy Department to reveal to its students that every philosophy is based, deep down, on a mere assumption. Students these days are seeking "truth" with more earnestness than ever before in my experience as a teacher. They specialize in philosophy in unprecedented numbers. Yet the Philosophy Department never tells them that their search for truth must always start and end with an arbitrary assumption. Because only the light side of every moon exists for the Philosophy Department, and because it dares not reveal the emptiness at the root of "truth", the Philosophy Department only half-educates its students. That is why so many of those who major in philosophy are, like all half-educated people, smug, suave, superficial.

Someone having a university *Education Department* in mind, said: "Those who can, do; those who can't, teach; and those who can neither do nor teach, teach Education." Though there are notable exceptions, it is ironic that the Department of Education offers the most universally boring courses and professors. The Education people have themselves to thank for this situation. Having established and maintained control of every state's educational system, they have set up certain standards for teachers. These standards invariably include a disproportionate number of courses in Education, and a correspondingly small number of courses in "solid" subjects. To meet the requirement for these numerous courses in Education, the Education Departments in nearly all universities have been forced to spread their material thinly through a multitude of courses. Material that could profitably be given in one course is spread through four or five courses. As a result, the courses are filled with trivia, well-known facts, self-evident platitudes; and the professors can teach them without having to know much, or demonstrate any important original ideas. This situation is especially deplorable because many of the students who take Education courses desire seriously to be of assistance to young people, and are willing to sacrifice a good deal in the way of money and luxury in order to help. They deserve better teaching.

CHAPTER ELEVEN

SELF-CURE FOR THE UNIVERSITY

Whose University Is It?

Everywhere in the world of higher education we hear an ominous murmur. It is suggested that college education should be reserved for "superior" students. President Case of Bard College is reported as saying that we should "weed out absolutely mercilessly those who do not respond fully" to the conditions now existing in American colleges. Professor Douglas Bush of Harvard says, "Education for all, however fine in theory, in practice leads ultimately to education for none. . . . The rising flood of students is very much like the barbarian invasions of the early Middle Ages." President Conant would like to see fewer students attending the universities, and proposes that "We do not expand our four-year colleges either as to number or as to size." And President Eisenhower's Committee on Education Beyond the High School says, ambiguously but with one eye on the increasing expenses of higher education, and the other eye on the theory that not everybody "deserves" to go to college: "If an unwelcome choice were required between preserving quality and expanding enrollments, then quality should be preferred."

This feeling that only the intellectual elite should be permitted to have the advantages of a higher education goes back even to that democrat Thomas Jefferson. Everyone, he thought, should have three years of schooling so as to learn how to read and write. From each elementary school, *only one boy* was to be selected to go on to one of twenty grammar schools in the state, and there be further educated for two years. Then, *only one boy* was to be selected each year from each of the twenty grammar schools to be allowed six more years of education. At the end of this six year period, one half the students remaining were to be sent to college for three years. Jefferson figured that this scheme would produce annually, in the entire state of Virginia, twenty high school graduates schooled at state expense, and only ten fit for college education. All the other pupils were to be dismissed as "rubbish."

The folly of Jefferson's low opinion of the intellectual capacities of the "rubbish" has been amply demonstrated. Today there is hardly a healthy child in the nation who is unable to absorb at least seven years of schooling, and only a small percentage who are unable to finish high school. In the same way, I am convinced that, a century or so from now, those educators who wish to reserve college for the intellectual elite will seem quite as unrealistic as Jefferson seems now. I am sure that the last-generation concept of education as a special privilege for the few will give way to ideas like those of young President Harold Taylor of Sarah Lawrence College who writes, "Education is for everyone. Let us have as many people in college as we can bring there. Let us accommodate our higher learning to the task of raising the intelligence of our population higher, not looking down on them from a disdainful height as if the educated minority were a separate breed." As for the carefully selected "superior" student, President Taylor goes on to say, "I am arguing that there are more and shinier fish in the sea than have ever been pulled out, and if we know how to fish, we can learn to throw a wider net."

Universities and their professors like to excuse their failures with large portions of their students by saying that the latter are "inferior," without much "brains" or "intelligence," and never should have gone to college in the first place. The universities and their professors think that by setting up more and more rigid standards of admission they will cull out the "inferior" minds. But the fact is, as was indicated in an earlier chapter of this book, all this culling does little good; the universities are still unsuccessful with a very large percentage of their students. But even if by some miracle of prophecy, the nature of which has not yet been revealed, the admissions committees *could* spot the intellectual elite, selection of them for the university and exclusion of the others would be unjustifiable.

In the first place, the students accepted would constitute the intellectual elite only according to the ideals of professors, and mostly education and psychology professors at that. Those ideals, as I have been subtly hinting in preceding chapters, may not be, in relation to the ultimate welfare of mankind, the wisest ideals imaginable.

In the next place, it must be obvious to everyone that there are so many kinds of "superiority" that the admissions committees are going to fall into a hopeless muddle if they try to choose the most superior possible of all available superiorities. Are they going to choose for college education the youth who can write a novel or the one who can build a bridge; the one who can get along with other people and influence public opinion or the one who can do calculus; the one who is a miracle man at horticulture or the one who is a miracle man at electronics; the one who is a shy specialist in entomology or the one who is the "well-rounded" president of his class and the maker of A's in all his subjects; the one who is a natural-born expert in languages or the one who is a precocious chemist?

A third argument against selection of only the "superior" for higher education is almost biological. What is considered superior and desirable in one age is not considered so in the next age, and the sought-after expert of today finds himself abandoned tomorrow. Fifty years ago, in the horse-and-buggy days, veterinarians were in great demand. Now imagine what would have happened to this nation if the colleges fifty years ago had declared that, in those "grim times," the very existence of the nation depended on the welfare of its livestock, and that all the students showing veterinary aptitudes should be admitted to college, and those interested in the new-fangled internal combustion engine or atomic physics or silly dreams like planetary rockets should obviously be excluded. Where would America be now? Just as animal life, in order to survive, must proliferate a constant variety of new forms during every geological period, with the virtual certainty that at least a few of the forms will be able to meet the constantly changing conditions of life, so education must produce a constant variety of intellectual forms. The admissions committees of our colleges are not able to select with any accuracy students who will be certain to do well in college during the next nine months. And how much more incompetent the committees must be in determining what kind of "superiority" will be in demand ten years or twenty years from now! The only salvation lies in the education of *everybody* to the limit of his ability in whatever field he finds himself most at home.

Not only does national salvation lie in educating everybody to the limit of his ability; realization of those principles that we have learned to call democratic lies in the same direction. In a democracy where the worth and the intrinsic dignity of every individual human being is held paramount, what else can we consistently do except see that every individual is given equal consideration and equal opportunity to develop himself to the best of his ability? We recognize that it is quite as wrong for the richest and most intelligent person in the nation to murder a mere nobody as it is for a mere nobody to murder the richest and most intelligent person. In the same way, it is quite as wrong for us to deny education to the merest nobody as it is to deny it to the richest and most intelligent person. Only when we decide to abandon democracy, may we embrace the doctrine of "higher education for the intellectual elite alone."

This does not mean, of course, that every person must be educated in exactly the same way. Equality does not mean identity. As President Harold Taylor says in the article already quoted, "Differences in kind and degree of intelligence do exist, and the university or college is only one formal institution through which an education can be obtained and human beings can learn." Nevertheless, human beings are enough alike, and the university or college is capable of so much variety and

flexibility, that most high school graduates can realize
their potentialities within university and college walls —
provided university and college make a serious effort to
cure themselves of all the really grave ills that beset them
today.

Never can any truly democratic American subscribe
to the heresy that the university and the college are
only for the select few, the destined leaders of society,
the young people proved by tests to have "superior intelligence." In its Report (1947), the President's Commission on Higher Education said:

> American colleges and universities must envision
> a much larger role for higher education in the na-
> tional life. They can no longer consider themselves
> merely the instrument for producing an intellectual
> elite; they must become the means by which every
> citizen, youth, and adult is enabled and encouraged
> to carry his education, formal and informal, as far
> as his native capacities permit.
>
> This conception is the inevitable consequence of
> the democratic faith; universal education is indis-
> pensable. . . . Education that liberates and en-
> nobles must be made equally available to all. Justice
> to the individual demands this; the safety and
> progress of the Nation depend upon it.

This very fine expression of democracy and American-
ism as applied to higher education may be contrasted
with that of a Danish educator who happened to be
visiting me not long ago. He had just come from inspect-
ing a Negro university in the South, where he had found
deplorably "low standards."

"To think," he said, "that people are given *degrees* for doing work like that!"

"Does it really matter?" I said. "Is not the important thing the fact that human beings are learning something, even if they are not learning much, that they are realizing whatever potentialities they have, even if their potentialities may not be great?"

"But a *degree!*"

My friend was speaking like a European, a North Teuton, and a Lutheran. To him education implied a struggle for a title by means of self-discipline and hard work. The degree is the thing. In America the degree should be nothing more than a child's trinket at the bottom of a box of educational cereal, a pleasing bauble to be had after the delightful and nourishing food has been consumed, but of no real importance.

The President's Commission made a "conservative estimate" that in 1947 "at least 49 per cent of our population has the mental ability" to go through junior college, and 32 per cent to go through a university. I do not know how these percentages were arrived at. But in my own experience, any student (with a few rare exceptions) who can master the first two years of college can master the last two years even more easily, *provided he has had good teaching in the first two years.* The Commission's estimate was very, very "conservative." In justice to the Commission, however, it must be said that it concluded that, if adequate educational opportunities had been fully available throughout early life to all persons from whom statistics were derived, this percentage would have been much higher. If every child were brought up in moderately comfortable economic circumstances, and were taught even moderately well through his public schooling, there is no doubt in my mind that at least 80 per cent of all high school graduates would be good college material.

Four Ideals

If our young people are to profit by university training, the universities must keep before them four ideals that very few of them maintain today.

The first of these is the democratic ideal which I have just been discussing. The American university must not become (as certain university presidents wish) the special preserve of an "intellectual elite," if anybody knows just who the intellectually elite are. The American university must be a service institution, an intellectual cafeteria, ready to serve all comers.

The second ideal is scientific. The university should subject itself to constant self-analysis and self-criticism. If the university were a psychological experiment carried on with white rats under laboratory conditions, the smug assumptions, the uncritical self-satisfaction, the contentment with all the basic but unquestioned premises on which the experiment depends would rule out the experiment in every respectable laboratory in the country. The universities must learn to exercise on themselves some of the rational judgment, the critical impartiality, and the untiring search for truth on which they are ever congratulating themselves.

The third ideal is Christian. The scientific ideal, the search after "Truth," is not sufficient. When Jesus of Nazareth said, "The truth shall make you free," he was referring to the truth of his own message — a message of love, compassion, sympathy, mercy, charity, kindness, humanity. No man can afford to pass by on the other side when a fellow human being (especially a young person) needs help; no man can afford to allow the letter to rule the spirit, to believe that man was made for the Sabbath instead of the Sabbath for man; no man can afford to become a stumbling block to them that are weak. It is not an accident that the poor and the ignorant of America, groping blindly but perhaps knowing instinctively, criticize the universities for being un-Christian; nor is it an accident that laborers, farmers, and the poor everywhere are suspicious of what they regard as university snobbery, class-superiority, and lack of sympathy for the underdog. The universities are guilty, by and large. They have defended so long the Truth of the Mind that they have almost forgotten that there is also a Truth of the Heart. Too many of their professors have become arrogant, self-important, impersonal, unhelpful, selfish, often cruel; and their administrations, forgetting the essential needs of individual human beings, wander bemused in a maze of rules, regulations, requirements, grade records, semester-hour records, test records, credit records, and IBM cards.

The British poet W. H. Davies wrote:

> Lord, I say nothing; I profess
> No faith in Thee nor Christ Thy Son.

But (he goes on to say) he will "follow Christ the man, In that humanity He taught." This, at any rate, the professors and the university administrations may do. If they don't do it, they can expect to remain the failures that they have become.

The final ideal is hard to define. It is akin to the Greek spirit and the Renaissance spirit. It is the spirit that can recognize the joy that comes from learning, engaging in new intellectual experiences, in new aesthetic experiments, in new discovery and fresh accomplishment. It is a sunny spirit, not dark and melancholy; it is joyous, not dour. Its followers have learned the magic of converting duty into delight, labor into love, study into creation, learning into adventure. This is, perhaps, of all these four ideals, the one that can be least spared, and also the one in which the universities and their professors are most deficient.

The Will to Teach Well

Some university administrators admit openly, and nearly all show by their practice, that they put little value on the art of teaching among their faculty. And the professors themselves often admit that they are not at all interested in teaching; sometimes they even boast about their bad teaching; seldom do they trouble themselves very much in order to perfect themselves as teachers.

How, then, is good teaching to be had on the university campus? There is no guaranteed answer to the question. It is well known, however, that nearly all people will do what they know is socially approved. Therefore, if in any university the trustees, the president, the department heads, and the more respected professors show (in any number of ways) that they think teaching important; and if the president and the department heads regularly give some tactful encouragement (a word of recognition, some campus honor, a raise in salary) to good teachers; and if all the university authorities continually stress in public speeches and announcements, and in private talks and written messages, that they are concerned that the faculty shall teach well — the faculty will soon desire to teach well. All that is required is the adoption of a definite and stated policy, and continual reminders to the faculty that it is a policy. A leaf may be taken here from the book of the propagandists and the public relations experts: people will believe anything, and do almost anything, if they are told to often enough and emphatically enough.

It may be argued that the will to teach well, even if it could be cultivated in the professors, is not sufficient, that good teachers are born, not made, that the road to hell is paved by people who have good will and nothing else. There is an element of truth in this. On the other hand, most professors are not slow witted. They can take advice about how to teach, they can follow instructions, they can learn at any rate not to make some of the most glaring errors. They can even learn (by a little self-psychiatry) to understand their own characters, and know how early experiences created in them certain maladjustments, a sense of insecurity, inferiority complexes, compensatory arrogance, fear and intolerance, and so on. All that is required is the incentive to understand, and the cure follows almost automatically. It is the task of the university authorities to create an atmosphere in which the professor will develop the incentive to make himself not so bad a teacher and not so objectionable a personality as he often is.

Teaching Teachers

A recently published study of university teaching, conducted by the University of Illinois, contains this polite understatement: "Many of the teachers in our colleges and universities are not equipped to do high-quality teaching." Then the study adds a very significant observation: "Although most other professions require an apprenticeship to give the individual needed experience in what to do with what he has, there is little or no provision made by our institutions of higher learning for instructors to learn how to teach."

Young instructors are hired *solely* on the basis of what they are supposed to know about a certain subject, not on the basis of their ability to teach it. If a young man or woman has made good grades in certain highly specialized graduate courses, and has written a dissertation proving himself a master of certain minute details about a fairly insignificant subject, he is hired to teach young people in the university. Nothing else is required of him. Even worse, he is often hired to teach the young while he is still a graduate student, even before he has made good grades in certain specialized courses, or written a dissertation. In either case, the chances are excellent that, before assuming his teaching duties, he has never before stood up in front of a class, never had any formal instruction in teaching, never had any helpful advice about teaching or the responsibilities of the teacher from either his department head or any other representative of the university administration. He is like a person who has been told, in a mechanic's shop, all about the workings of an internal combustion engine, and is then placed in an airplane pilot's seat, and told to take the plane up and fly it. In this case, tragedy for the pilot is almost inevitable; in the case of the young instructor, the tragedy befalls his students.

Skeptics may say that the art of teaching cannot be taught, that teachers, like poets, are born and not made. This also is partly true. Nevertheless, if the entire university atmosphere made the young instructor feel that teaching is considered important on his particular campus, and if the four ideals of higher education mentioned earlier in this chapter were discussed with the young instructor, and if every department head gave a brief course (two or three weeks) in which he told his young instructors how to solve some of the problems and answer some of the questions that always arise in classes of that particular department, young teachers could learn, at any rate, how not to be really bad teachers, even if they never learned to be really good ones. Again, the chief prerequisite for good teaching is the will, by everybody concerned, to have good teaching.

The research professor who is interested only in a stream of published "papers" with his name on them will argue that good teaching takes too much time away from research. But this is not true. Having the will to teach well does not take time; keeping before one the four ideals mentioned earlier does not take time. It takes no more time to avoid being sarcastic, arrogant, ill-tempered, egotistical, self-important, intolerant, and opinionated in class than it does to be all those things. It takes no more time to put into practice a few general rules of public speaking (previously learned in half a day) than it does not to practice them. It takes no more time to correct a student's opinion politely than to correct it boorishly. It takes no more time to laugh and show that one has a sense of humor than it does to be Puritanically solemn, or imitate a robot in class. It takes no more time to speak in plain and simple English than it does to speak in polysyllabic technical jargon that bewilders the students. It takes no more time to make out fair and representative examinations than it does to make out tricks and catch questions. It takes no more time to nod and smile at a student one meets on the campus than to pass him with a cold and unseeing stare. It takes no more time to hold conferences in a friendly, genial spirit than it does to hold them with impersonal formality. It takes no more time to talk with students on the campus, in the lunchroom, in the bookstore, at the theatre, and anywhere else out of class with the easy familiarity that a kind older man ought to have for any young person, than it does to maintain a stiff officer-private relationship. It takes no more time to be a little warm and human about minor student infractions (a paper a day late, a class cut on the day of the big game, a lesson unprepared when a boy's best girl was in town the night before, and so on) than it does to be harsh and unyielding.

It may take a little more time to work up clearly organized instead of rambling and incoherent lectures, to make clear instead of vague assignments, to think up original and pertinent illustrations and exercises rather than depending strictly on the textbook, to think up ways to help the students study better instead of just leaving them to sink or swim, but it doesn't take *much* more time. The pressure of research is only an excuse for self-ishness or a cover-up for psychological inadequacy.

Teaching Students

It is said that when Sir Walter Raleigh went to the block, he was told by the executioner to kneel down so that his head would face the east. "What matter," answered Sir Walter, "how the head lies, so long as the heart is right?"

It is much the same way with teaching. If the heart is right, good teaching will follow. Students and parents, taxpayers and benefactors, university administrators and the country as a whole, should demand professors whose hearts are right.

This may sound like an unrealistic note of idealism in "these grim times." But I should like to call attention here to a rather extensive report made a few years ago by the researchers of *Business Week*, hardly an unrealistic or idealistic publication. The report covered work done by the University of Michigan Survey Research Center, and was financed partly by the Office of Naval Research, and partly by business concerns. The researchers concentrated on the thousands of semi-skilled clerical employees of the Prudential Life Insurance Company. Most of these employees are organized into crews of 10 to 25 people working under a supervisor. Of course, these conditions do not duplicate those in a university classroom; but there is a certain similarity. Besides, it is the role of the supervisor (corresponding to that of the teacher) which is significant.

It was found that the supervisors were of two quite distinct types — close supervisors and loose supervisors.

> The close supervisors tend to have rather cold personalities. They consider that their principal responsibility is to get out a high volume of work. They feel a close identification with the company. They put a lot of pressure on their people for output. . . .
>
> The loose supervisors . . . aren't very company-minded. They take a personal interest in their girls on and off the job. They devote most of their supervisory effort to keeping the girls interested and happy. . . .
>
> The loose, people-minded supervisors have the most productive crews.

The close, production-minded supervisors . . . don't get the production.

In interpreting these results, which are "just the opposite of what one might expect," the reporters go on to say:

> A girl is productive if she wants a great deal, and can find an outlet for her needs by working hard.

> For most of the girls, the significant need . . . is for interesting challenging work. The warm permissive supervisor stimulates this need; she gets her girls interested, raises their aspirations. Wanting more out of their work experience, they put more into it.

If these findings have any relation to the process of college education (and I think they do), they show that the professor whose "heart is right," who is more interested in human beings than in rules, regulations, cold knowledge, "maintaining the standards of the university," and keeping the educational organization smoothly functioning is likely to be a more successful teacher than his opposite.

A professor whose heart is right will not wish to make the university a place where the only young people who are welcome are the "intellectual elite." He will regard the university as a place where almost every young person in the nation should have an opportunity to discover something of value to that young person individually. The professor will not regard most people as mere chaff, and only a handful as solid grain; rather, he will take exactly the reverse attitude. If students do not learn much in his classes, he will not blame them, but himself;

and he will try to improve himself as a teacher. He will feel a profound moral obligation to these young people in his classes; he will no more leave them to sink or swim, as best they may, in the ocean of knowledge than he would walk off and leave a child drowning in the surf.

He will look askance at those puzzle-tests which pretend to evaluate human nature, with all its manifold complexities, in terms of arithmetic. As a matter of fact, he will realize that, except in uncommon cases of abnormality, evaluation of human nature is usually unsafe and unsound. If he gives tests at all, they will be attempts to discover young people who have imagination, creativeness, sensitivity, insight, a sense of social and human responsibility, courage, originality, and a dozen other such qualities, and no tests at all for so-called "intelligence" and no attempt at arithmetical evaluation (any more than one can evaluate arithmetically the results of a Rorschach test), but only at description.

Once the student is in the university, the professor will be less interested in making the student learn some law or fact, than in making him *want* to learn. The student who *wants* to learn is the only one who can be successfully taught. Knowing this, the professor will not try to frighten or shame his students into learning, holding over them the club of grades and a sense of duty; he will try to show them how delightful it is to learn. He will be able to show them this if he too delights in learning, and also delights in stimulating others to delight.

Nor will the professor be so lost in rules and regulations that he will forget that any human being is worth more than all the rules and regulations. Perhaps right here is the sum and substance of what makes a good teacher. It is a constant and overpowering awareness, during every moment that he gives to teaching, that he is dealing with human beings, and that they automatically deserve his help, his respect, and his affection.

SELECTED BIBLIOGRAPHY

In a book of personal reflections such as this, elaborate documentation would be misleading and inappropriate. Nevertheless, the reader may wish to know the sources of some of the more controversial and less obvious statements and statistics that have been taken from other writers for use in this book. The following brief bibliography may help him:

Anonymous. "What Makes them *Want* to Work?" *Business Week*, August 28, 1954, pp. 119-31.

Anderson, John R. "Do College Students *Lack* Motivation?" *Personnel and Guidance Journal*, 33 (1954): 209-210.

Bush, Douglas. "The Humanities," *Educational Review*, 36 (1955): 64-69.

Conant, James Bryant. *Education in a Divided World*. Cambridge, Massachusetts: Harvard University Press, 1948.

Cox, Catherine M. *The Early Mental Traits of 300 Geniuses.* Stanford, California: Stanford University Press, 1926.

Eells, Walter Crosby. *College Teachers and College Teaching.* Atlanta, Georgia: Southern Regional Education Board, 1957.

Garnett, Raymond Loren. *Some Factors in College Success.* Columbia, Missouri: Privately printed, 1931. (Ph.D. thesis, University of Missouri.)

Hale, William Harlan. "The Quizmasters Fasten on to Higher Education," *Reporter,* 13 (October 6, 1955): 14-20.

Harris, Daniel. *The Relation of College Grades to Some Factors Other than Intelligence.* New York: Columbia University Press, 1931.

Heaton, Kenneth L., and Vivian Weedon. *The Failing Student.* Chicago: University of Chicago Press, 1940.

Hepner, H. W. *Psychology Applied to Life and Work.* New York: Prentice-Hall, 1950.

Hollinshead, Byron. *Who Should Go to College?* New York: Columbia University Press, 1952.

Hook, Sidney. "Modern Education and its Critics." An address delivered at Chicago, February 12, 1954; reprinted in *Seventh Yearbook of the American Association of Colleges for Teachers of Education,* 1954.

Jefferson, Thomas. *Notes on the State of Virginia* (1784).

Jersild, Arthur T. *The Psychology of Adolescence.* New York: Columbia University Press, 1957.

Knapp, Robert H., and Joseph J. Greenbaum. *The Younger American Scholar.* Chicago: University of Chicago Press and Wesleyan University Press, 1953.

Lazarsfeld, Paul F. *The Academic Mind.* Glencoe, Illinois: Free Press, 1958.

Riley, John W., *et al. The Student Looks at his Teacher.* New Brunswick, New Jersey: Rutgers University Press, 1950.

Rogers, F. M. "University Teaching." An address printed in *Proceedings of the Second General Conference of the International Association of Universities, September 19-24, 1955.*

Russell, Bertrand. *Education and the Good Life.* New York: Boni and Liveright, 1926.

Russell, Bertrand. "The Functions of a Teacher," *Unpopular Essays.* New York: Simon and Schuster, 1950.

Salley, Ruth E., and Ruth G. Weintraub. "Student Records of Entrance and Graduation," *School and Society,* 69 (1949): 404-406.

Schneider, Franz. *Students Examine their Professors.* Berkeley, California: Pestalozzi Press, 1939.

Smith, C. Page. "The Sins of Higher Education," *Journal of Higher Education,* 26 (1955): 31-36, 58.

Smith, C. Page. "Human Time and the College Student," *Journal of Higher Education,* 28 (1957): 70-74, 116-17.

Stroup, Herbert. "The Intentions of Student-Activities Systems," *Journal of Higher Education,* 27 (1956): 256-63, 290.

Taylor, Harold. "Education for What and for Whom?" *School and Society,* 83 (1956): 39-43.

Travers, R. M. W. *Educational Measurement.* New York: Macmillan, 1955.

Tunis, John R. *Was College Worth While?* New York: Harcourt, Brace, 1936.

Whitehead, Alfred North. *The Aims of Education and Other Essays.* New York: Macmillan, 1929.